PANZERS AT WAR

MICHAEL &
GLADYS GREEN

ZENITH
PRESS

DEDICATION

At the request of Dr. Wolfgang Sterner, a German army tank commander in World War II,
the authors dedicate this book to all of the German tankers of World War II.

First published in 2005 by Zenith Press, an imprint of MBI Publishing Company, Galtier Plaza, Suite 200, 380 Jackson Street, St. Paul, MN 55101-3885 USA

The information in this book is true and complete to the best of our knowledge. All recommendations are made without any guarantee on the part of the author or Publisher, who also disclaim any liability incurred in connection with the use of this data or specific details.

This publication has been prepared solely by MBI Publishing Company and is not approved or licensed by any other entity. We recognize that some words, model names, and designations mentioned herein are the property of the trademark holder. We use them for identification purposes only. This is not an official publication.

Zenith Press titles are also available at discounts in bulk quantity for industrial or sales-promotional use. For details write to Special Sales Manager at MBI Publishing Company, Galtier Plaza, Suite 200, 380 Jackson Street, St. Paul, MN 55101-3885 USA.

ISBN-13: 978-0-7603-2152-2
ISBN-10: 0-7603-2152-3

Editor: Steve Gansen

Printed in China

On the frontispiece: A *Panzerbefehlswagen*, a command-tank version of the Panther tank series. It features two extra radios and two additional antennas, one mounted on the turret roof and the other on the rear of the hull. *Thomas Anderson*

On the title page: Tiger I tank, built in February 1943, parked next to Pz.Kpfw. III Ausf. L, built in 1942. *Tank Museum–Bovington*

On the front cover: The world's only operational Tiger 1 tank being driven on the grounds of the Tank Museum at Bovington in the summer of 2004. *Tank Museum-Bovington*
Inset: Restored Pz.Kpfw III armed with long-barreled 50mm main gun. *Tank Museum-Bovington*

About the authors:
Michael and Gladys Green are freelance writers, researchers, and photographers who specialize in military, transportation, and law enforcement subjects, with more than 50 books to their credit. The Greens live in Northern California.

CONTENTS

ACKNOWLEDGMENTS

IN ADDITION TO THOSE WHOSE NAMES ARE MENTIONED in the text or photo credits of this book, special thanks are also due to very helpful staffs of the U.S. Army's Patton Museum of Cavalry and Armor, Fort Knox, Kentucky; the Tank Museum, Bovington, England; Wehrtechnische Studiensammlung (WTS), Koblenz, Germany; and the U.S. Army Ordnance Museum, Aberdeen, Maryland. Individuals that made an extra effort in assisting the authors include Thomas Anderson, George Bradford (who supplied many of the line drawings for this book), Lesley Delsing, Frank Schulz, Randy Talbot, Dean and Nancy Kleffman, Richard Byrd, Dick Hunnicutt, Ron Hare, Jim Brown, and Richard Cox.

INTRODUCTION

WHILE THE GERMAN ARMY DEPENDED UPON MASSES of infantry and utilized horse-drawn transport throughout the war, when you think of the World War II *Wehrmacht*, you think of blitzkrieg, lightning war, and the panzers that spearheaded the Nazi offensives. *Panzers at War* will introduce you to the world of wartime German armor, the panzers.

Although Germany was restricted from manufacturing tanks by the terms of the Versailles Treaty in the years following World War I, the German army used wooden and canvas mockups of tanks placed on civilian automobiles to simulate armored vehicles in their training and in the development of their war-fighting doctrine. This helped provide a sound base for the evolution of the German armor force, the *panzertruppen*, with the rise of Hitler.

The 1930s would see the manufacture of the first German panzers starting with light tanks such as the *Panzer-Kampfwagen* I and II. (*Panzer* means armored and *kampfwagen* means fighting vehicle. It is typically abbreviated Pz.Kpfw.) The Pz.Kpfw. I, finding itself outgunned, had a less than auspicious combat debut during the Spanish Civil War (1936–1939). German innovation continued, however, leading to the installation of 20mm automatic cannons in the Pz.Kpfw. II.

By the beginning of World War II the Germans had also developed a medium tank, the Pz.Kpfw. III. Initially fielded with a 37mm high-velocity cannon augmented with three 7.92mm machine guns, combat experience proved the need for a more capable main gun, and a 50mm high-velocity cannon began to appear in the fall of 1940. Continuous improvement was a hallmark of German armor as well as an expedient use of often limited assets; by June 1942 the model N (Ausf. N) of the Pz.Kpfw. III series entered into production.

Concurrent with the Mark III, a larger, heavier medium tank, the Pz.Kpfw. IV was in development as an escort or support vehicle for the smaller panzers, the Marks I–III. For this role it was fitted with a short-barreled, low-velocity 75mm main gun. Once again, combat (this time in France and Russia) demonstrated the need for a higher velocity main gun, and Pz.Kpfw. IV Ausf. F2s equipped with a long-barreled, high-velocity weapon began to appear in 1942. By war's end, the total number of Pz.Kpfw. IV–series tanks numbered over 9,000, making it the most numerous of the German tanks to see service during World War II.

Experience in Russia proved that the German panzer lineup was no match for the Red Army's T-34 medium tank. This resulted in the development and fielding of a new, heavier medium tank, originally designated the Pz.Kpfw. V Panther (Mark V). With substantially thicker armor and a first-rate high-velocity cannon, the Panther proved to be a formidable opponent for any Allied tank. It entered German service in limited quantities in time for Operation Citadel (*Operation Zitadelle*) in the summer of 1943—along with the most-feared tank of World War II, the Tiger.

The groundwork for what would become the Tiger I heavy tank began in 1941. The German army ordnance department specifications called for a vehicle weighing up to 45 tons that would be armed with the superlative 88mm dual-purpose high-velocity gun. The Tiger I began production in August 1942. Even with the fielding of the American high-velocity 90mm main gun in the T36 tank destroyer and M28 Pershing towards the end of the war, the Tiger tank was still king when it came to slugging it out toe-to-toe on the armored battlefield.

While this volume makes no claim to be a definitive history of the development and use of the panzers in World War II, *Panzers at War* provides a concise introduction to and broad overview of wartime German armor. With extensive photographic coverage of Pz.Kpfw. I–VI accompanied by a detailed text, it is the authors' hope that both those new to the study of World War II as well as more seasoned experts will find a satisfying experience in these pages.

Pictured on display at the U.S. Army Ordnance Museum is a British army Mark IV tank from World War I. The British army classified Mark IV tanks armed with 57mm guns as males, while those armed only with machine guns became known as females. This particular vehicle appears to be female, based on the gun-mount arrangement. *Michael Green*

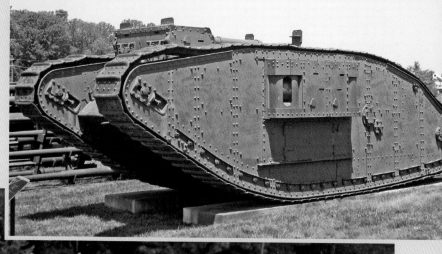

Taking part in a public display at the German Tank Museum is a Pz.Kpfw. II Ausf. F, the final production vehicle in the series. A key external spotting feature of the Ausf. F was the dummy driver's visor mounted to the left of the real driver's visor and partially hidden by the spare road wheel attached to the lower front hull of the tank. *Thomas Anderson*

CHAPTER ONE
LIGHT TANKS

THE BRITISH ARMY WAS THE first to employ tanks in battle during World War I (1914–1918). Their objective in the Battle of the Somme on September 15, 1916, was to break through the German army's defensive lines in France. While this "tank debut" was not an overwhelming success, the fear that the British tanks inspired among the defending German soldiers encouraged the British generals to ask for more of them.

The turretless British tank employed in battle that day was designated the Mark I. It had a crew of eight men and weighed about 28 tons (25.4 metric tons). Power came from a gasoline engine that gave it a top speed of four miles per hour (6.44 kilometers per hour). Armor protection on the vehicle consisted of steel armor plate no thicker than 0.4 inch (10 millimeters). The Mark I was armed with two 57mm guns, one mounted on either side of the vehicle's long, rhomboidal-shaped hull, and five machine guns. By the end of World War I, the British army had placed into service an improved model designated the Mark IV, which featured slightly thicker armor protection.

The French army had also become very interested in tanks early in the war. However, their first tanks did not go into battle until the spring of 1917. Their first combat engagement during the Nivelle Offensive suffered from poor tactics and the primitive nature of the vehicles, which were very vulnerable to high-explosive (HE) rounds from German artillery pieces. Despite their initial disappointment, the French army continued to fund tank development.

The German and Austrian armies did not start developing their own tanks until they saw the potential of British tanks on the battlefield. At that time, the more far-thinking individuals within the German army convinced their more conservative counterparts to begin developmental work on their own tanks. Their first tank was a 30-ton (27.2 metric tons) turretless vehicle code-named A7V. The code name derived from the government department responsible for its design and construction—the *Allgemeines Kriegdepartment 7. Abteilung Verkehrswesen*. This translates to the General War Department 7th Traffic Section.

The A7V first appeared on the battlefield during the final German offensive of the war on March 21, 1918. It featured a single 57mm main gun and six machine guns. Power came from two Daimler-Benz gasoline engines

that gave the tank a top speed of 8 miles per hour (13 kilometers per hour). The tank had a crew of 18 men and could carry four more when required. It was 26 feet 3 inches (8 meters) long, had a width of 10 feet (3 meters), and was 10 feet 10 inches (3.3 meters) tall.

The Imperial German Army took into service between 15 and 35 A7Vs before the war ended in November of 1918. Plans to deploy a new generation of light and heavy tanks in early 1919 never came to fruition.

To prevent the German army from being able to threaten Europe again, the Western Allies forced Germany to sign the Versailles Treaty in June of 1919. The provisions of the treaty limited Germany to an army of no more than 100,000 men, precluded the possession of tanks, and allowed only a small number of armored cars for internal security duties.

POST–WORLD WAR I GERMAN TANK DEVELOPMENT

Even as the post-World War I German army, called the *Reichsheer*, was in the process of selling or destroying the few remaining tanks in its inventory, German generals began planning ways of subverting the Versailles Treaty restrictions to continue tank development. In its endeavor to rebuild itself once again into a formidable military force, the *Reichsheer* was fortunate to find itself

under the able stewardship of Hans von Seeckt, commander-in-chief between 1919 and 1926, who laid the groundwork for a revitalized German army.

Seeckt set about the task of reorganizing the German army by absorbing the lessons of World War I and incorporating the benefits of tanks and airplanes. Seeckt wanted to return mobility to the German army, so he rewrote the army's manuals and field service regulations. He incorporated war games into the training plans as an important tool by which the new army leaders could gain practical experience in the new methods of fighting without the costly learning curve inherent in real war.

The core of Seeckt's tactical thinking was the traditional German manner of waging war. The main thrust of any offensive operation was, as always, the infantry. Orders were to be short and direct, leaving a local commander to decide the best tactics to employ in his mission—a concept known as *Auftragstaktik*. Pushing forward, the unit would search for the weak points in the enemy lines to allow for follow-on forces to exploit the breakthrough, turn the enemy's flank, and envelop them.

Even though his tactics were steeped in tradition, Seeckt was open to new ideas that could improve the German army. He was well aware of the crucial role that tanks would play in future conflicts. Seeckt correctly deduced that the technical aspects and tactics were both important to mission success. He and many other senior German army officers believed that the "army's strength would lie in mobility, guaranteed by a large contingent of cavalry, a

This very nicely restored Pz.Kpfw. I Ausf. A featuring an early-World War II paint scheme is driving out of the German Tank Museum for a public display. The tank driver is Kurt Fischer, who helped to restore the vehicle to running condition. He gained his initial experience on the vehicle by serving in them in World War II. *Thomas Anderson*

well-conditioned infantry, and a full complement of motorized and mechanized units."

As tank technology continued to improve in the 1920s, Seeckt realized that cavalry was becoming a relic of the past. In 1924, he wrote in a German army manual that he foresaw a time when tanks were perfected, and "they would be able to fight in mobile warfare." One of the more influential writers on armored tactics in Germany during the interwar period was Ernst Volckheim. In 1924, he described what would become armored doctrine for the German army in his books *Tanks in Modern Warfare* and *German Tanks in the World War*. He stressed that tanks were primarily infantry-support weapons and went on to predict, like Seeckt, that future tanks would be faster, more mobile, and able to function independent of the infantry, cavalry, and other formations. Volckheim's views on using tanks as antitank weapons, and as command-and-control posts by installing radios in all vehicles, were popular with the German army.

In 1926, the last year of Seeckt's command, the German army conducted their largest training maneuvers since World War I. Lacking real tanks, the German army mounted canvas and sheet metal mockups of tanks on wheeled vehicles. By the end of the training maneuvers, the German army's Third Cavalry Division reported to headquarters that "battle without tanks is obsolete."

Despite his departure from the army, Seeckt's legacy included the reorganization of the German army, the rewriting of military regulations, and a new emphasis on offensive tactical doctrine. These contributions, along with the effectiveness of his training concepts, would remain keystones in the structure of the German army for many years.

Austrian General Ludwig von Eimannsberger, Colonel Heinz Guderian, and other open-minded army strategists expanded upon Seeckt's conceptual framework to define the role that tanks would play in future wars. Eimannsberger strongly believed that tank units should never attack by themselves. Rather, they should attack in a combined-arms formation with infantry, artillery, and aircraft in support. He also believed that tanks should attack in concentration, using their speed to punch through enemy lines, with follow-on formations exploiting gaps in the defense to attack the enemy's flank and rear areas.

Rolling out of the German Tank Museum for a public display is their restored Pz.Kpfw. I Ausf. A. Details of the rear engine compartment are clearly visible, as are the vision ports in the rear of the tank's turret and superstructure. The tank weighs 5.7 tons (5.4 metric tons). *Thomas Anderson*

Eimannsberger's theories, like those of Guderian, followed the armored doctrinal tactics that were widely accepted by the Germany military at that time.

Recently, historians have corrected the record on Guderian's contribution to the development of the armored doctrine in the German army. His major theoretical work, the book titled *Achtung-Panzer*, appeared two years after the establishment of the panzer force in 1935 and merely repeated many of the same themes that other armor advocates, German and foreign, had written prior to his own work. His main contribution to the armored doctrine of the German army in World War II was his maxim, *Klotzen, nicht Kleckern*, roughly translated as "strike

concentrated, not dispersed." Although many German armor officers of the time already agreed with this principle, Guderian's statement solidified the tactical concepts of mass and concentration practiced by the German army's tank units in the early part of World War II.

Between 1926 and 1932, the German army secretly commissioned a group of German companies to design and build a small number of experimental light and medium tanks. The funding for both light and medium tanks reflected uncertainty about the developmental approach. Some in the German army favored medium tanks that could accommodate a large variety of weapons and would have the ability to carry more armor. The majority tended to believe that much smaller and cheaper light tanks made more sense for the German army despite their lack of firepower and armor protection, since they had better mobility and could overwhelm an enemy by force of numbers. In 1930, one German army officer wrote that armies should build large numbers of small and cheap light tanks, but support them in battle with a number of better-armored and -armed medium tanks. The German army eventually adopted this approach.

Another reason that many in the German army favored small, inexpensive light tanks was that German industry lacked the experience and infrastructure to design and build large numbers of medium tanks. It was clear to the German army that they would have to make do with light tanks until German industry could gear up to build medium tanks. One reason for the infrastructure gap was the stock market crash of 1929, which seriously depressed the worldwide economy.

THE BEGINNINGS OF A NEW LIGHT TANK

In 1930, the German army's *Waffenamt* (ordnance department) selected Krupp to begin design work on a new armored light-tank chassis that would be suitable for both reconnaissance and self-propelled weapon-carrier roles. Krupp borrowed design features from a very small British army turretless light tank designed and built by the British firm of Carden-Lloyd. The two-man tank armed with a single machine gun first appeared in British army service in the late 1920s. Because of its diminutive size, it was generally referred to as a "tankette" in its day rather than a light tank.

Krupp failed to deliver on its promise to have an armored chassis ready for evaluation by June of 1931. A full year past the deadline, the new chassis still was not ready for evaluation. In July of 1932, the German army officer overseeing the project threatened to bypass Krupp altogether and buy tracked vehicles directly from

Belonging to the Military Vehicle Technology Foundation, located in California, this unrestored Pz.Kpfw. I Ausf. A was acquired in trade with the Canadian Army Museum. It features a four-cylinder, air-cooled Krupp gasoline engine that produced 60 horsepower. The vehicle commander acted as both gunner and loader. *Michael Green*

This picture shows the interior of the Pz.Kpfw. I Ausf. A belonging to the Military Vehicle Technology Foundation. The driver's seat is missing from this vehicle. Visible are the driver's controls, instrument panel, and, in the right-hand corner of the picture, the seat for the vehicle commander.
Michael Green

Carden-Lloyd, then owned by the British firm, Vickers. This threat seemed to have the desired effect on Krupp management, and that same month they delivered their first vehicle, code-named the *Landwirtschaftlicher Schlepper* (farm tractor). In German documents this was usually abbreviated as La.S.

THE FIRST SERIES PRODUCTION GERMAN TANK APPEARS

By the end of 1934, as Krupp gained experience with the production of steel armor plate and the mounting of weapons on tracked vehicles, the La.S. had evolved into the German army's first post-World War I tank. The original German army designation for the new light tank was the *Krupp-Traktor*. In April of 1936, the new tank received its military designation, the Pz.Kpfw. I Ausf. A (Sd.Kfz. 101).

The abbreviation Pz.Kpfw. stands for *PanzerKampfwagen* (armored fighting vehicle or tank). *Panzer* means armor or tank. Examples of its use are *Panzer-Armee* (armored army), and *Panzer-Abteilung* (armored battalion).

The abbreviation *Ausf.* stands for the German word *Ausführung* and refers to a specific model. The letter following *Ausf.* represented the model improvements in alphabetical sequence. This nomenclature system was replaced in early 1942 by one in which models of tanks

were supposed to be assigned the first letter of the civilian firms that designed them.

The abbreviation *Sd.Kfz.* stands for *Sonderkraftfahrzeug*, which means "special motor vehicle" and refers to the vehicle's ordnance inventory number.

The wartime Western Allies used the term "Mark" or its abbreviation "Mk." followed by a number, normally in a Roman numeral (I-VI), to describe various German tanks. In Soviet army documents the abbreviation Mk. became "T."

PZ.KPFW. I AUSF. A: DESCRIPTION

Tanks carry their own portable roads, called tracks. The tanks lay these tracks down in front of themselves and then pick them up as they moves away. The tracks are belts made up of interlocking track links (or shoes) connected by steel pins.

Drive sprockets, one on either side of the hull, receive their power from a tank's engine by way of the transmission. Large gears in the final drives reduce the transmission speed and increase the torque at the sprockets. The tracks are lifted off the ground at the rear of the vehicle after the rubber-tired or steel-rimmed road-wheels have driven over them. The tracks are under the control of the sprockets, which deliver the "tractive effort" between the tank and the ground.

Looking into the turret of the Pz.Kpfw. I Ausf. A belonging to the Military Vehicle Technology Foundation, the receivers of the two deactivated 7.92mm machine guns are visible. Missing from this particular vehicle is the 2.5-power telescopic sight located between the two machine guns, which provided the vehicle commander a 28-degree field of view. *Michael Green*

The components external to the hull (final drives, sprockets, idler wheels, tracks, and road wheels) make up a tank's *running gear*. The idler wheels, one for each track at the front of the vehicle (for rear-drive configurations) or at the rear (for front-drive configurations), reverse the direction of the tracks at the un-powered end of the vehicle. Most idler spindles are adjustable in position so that they can increase or decrease track tension. Tight tracks have high rolling resistance and shortened lives. Loose tracks are more easily lost to misguiding (thrown tracks).

Tank road wheels connect to the tank's hull by a suspension system that isolates the hull from rough terrain. The suspension protects the running gear from high forces and makes the ride tolerable for the crew. The addition of heavy dampers (shock absorbers) helps minimizes pitching and rolling of the hull.

The suspension system on the Pz.Kpfw. I Ausf. A consisted of five rubber-tired road wheels on each side. The rear (fifth) road wheel acted as the idler. The drive sprockets were located at the front of the hull. The front road wheels on either side of the vehicle's hull were independently sprung on coil springs. Large hydraulic shock absorbers were connected in parallel with the springs. The remaining road wheels were set in articulated pairs that mounted on a single arm pivoted at the center, which connected to leaf springs. A large exterior horizontal steel girder acted as a reinforcing beam and the attachment point for the last four road wheels. Three hull-mounted rollers supported the upper return strand of track.

The 5.9-ton (5.35 metric tons) Pz.Kpfw. I Ausf. A was powered by a Krupp-designed and -built air-cooled, four-cylinder gasoline-powered engine that delivered up to a maximum of 60 horsepower and was located in the rear of the vehicle's hull. A driveline connected the engine output to the transmission in the front. The top speed of the Pz.Kpfw. I Ausf. A was 23 miles per hour (37 kilometers per hour). With a full load of fuel, the tank had a maximum on-road operational of about 90 miles (145 kilometers).

The two-man crew consisted of a driver who sat in the front of the hull and a vehicle commander who also acted as the gunner. The commander station's seat was suspended from the small, hand-powered turret. Turret armament was two side-by-side-mounted 7.92mm machine guns, which could be fired together or separately. The vehicle commander communicated with the driver by way of a voice tube.

A tank's superstructure is the part of the vehicle's armored body that extends up from the hull and upon which a rotating weapon-armed turret is mounted. Modern tanks no longer have superstructures and consist of only a hull and turret. The German word for superstructure is *Panzerkastenoberteil*, while turret is *Turm*. Rather than the word *hull*, the Germans often used the term *Fahrgestell*, which translates to chassis.

The tank commander/gunner of the Pz.Kpfw. I Ausf. A entered and exited the vehicle through an overhead hatch in the turret. A 2.5-power optical sight was located

PzKpfw I Ausf. B (Sd Kfz 101)

Serving with the Pz-Lehr-Abt. c. 1936
Early Production

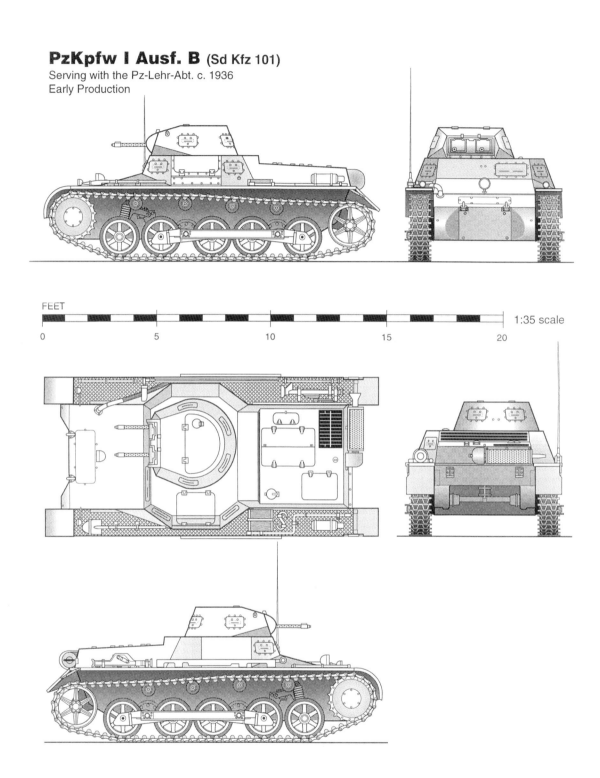

A number of design changes to the original Pz.Kpfw. I Ausf. A resulted in a designation change to Pz.Kpfw. I Ausf. B. The biggest change to the tank's design resulted from the mounting of a larger and more powerful liquid-cooled Maybach engine in place of the original air-cooled Krupp engine. The Krupp designers lengthened and enlarged the vehicle's rear hull compartment to accommodate the new engine, as seen in this five-view line drawing. *George Bradford*

On display at the U.S. Army Ordnance Museum is a German army Pz.Kpfw. I Ausf. B light tank. External spotting features of the vehicle, compared to the original Pz.Kpfw. I Ausf. A, are the five road wheels per hull side (the Ausf. A had only four per side) and the raised rear idler wheel. The rubber-rimmed road wheels were made from aluminum, and the rubber-rimmed idler wheel from cast steel. *Michael Green*

between the side-by-side turret-mounted machine guns. Armored flaps protected four vision ports in the tank's turret. The driver entered and exited the vehicle through a pair of hinged armored doors on the side of the super-structure. The maximum armor thickness on the new light tank was only 0.52 inch (13 millimeters), which only protected the vehicle against small arms fire and fragments.

The German army brought in Maschinenfabrik Augsburn Nürnberg (MAN), Henschel, Daimler-Benz, and a number of other companies to help Krupp, who worked in conjunction with the German firm of Grusonwerk (Krupp-Gruson) to meet the Pz.Kpfw. I Ausf. A delivery schedules. The German manufacturing consortium produced more than 1,000 Pz.Kpfw. I Ausf. A vehicles between 1935 and 1936.

PZ.KPFW. I AUSF. A: IN CONTEXT

The development and large-scale manufacture of the Pz.Kpfw. I Ausf. A coincided with the rise in power of Adolph Hitler and the Nazi Party, beginning in 1933. In February of 1934, Hitler told the German Army's top generals that he wanted them to be ready to conduct a defensive war within four years and an offensive war within eight years. That same month, Hitler visited the German army's ordnance testing ground for the first time and observed a training exercise that included a number of Pz.Kpfw. I Ausf. A light tanks and prototypes of the Ausf. B. Hitler was so impressed with the light tanks that he proclaimed, "That's what I need. That's what I want to have."

A small group of German army Pz.Kpfw. I Ausf. B light tanks and their crews are pictured taking cover next to a farmer's haystack during a pre-World War II training exercise. The crews have covered their vehicles with straw from the haystack. The horizontally mounted muffler on the rear of the Pz.Kpfw. I in the foreground marks it as an Ausf. B, since the Ausf. A had a small muffler mounted on either rear hull fender. *Patton Museum*

Hitler's sudden interest in tanks quickly led to an increase in tank development and manufacture. Hitler would eventually become deeply involved in the design and construction of German tanks, much to the dismay of the German army.

By March of 1935, Hitler was so confident in his growing military might and the lack of resolve by other European governments to stop his armament buildup that he announced to the world that Germany was no longer bound by the restrictions of the Versailles Treaty and was tripling the size of its army. With Hitler as the supreme leader (*führer*) of Germany, the German army became known as the *Heer*. The German word *Wehrmacht* would now encompass all German armed forces.

The Pz.Kpfw. I Ausf. A first took part in large-scale training maneuvers in 1936. By the following year, the German army had conducted the largest training exercise held in Germany since the end of World War I, involving over 160,000 men and 830 tanks. This was also the first time that the German army's newly formed panzer divisions would be put through their paces with tactical air support.

The first three panzer divisions of the German army were formed in October of 1935, and had a table of organization and equipment (TO&E) calling for 561 tanks each. German industry, however, never could manage to supply the quantities required. Two more panzer divisions appeared in 1938, and another one early the following year. These six panzer divisions helped to spearhead the invasion of Poland on September 1, 1939, which officially started World War II. The tank crews belonged to the elite of the German army—the *Panzertruppen* (armored troops). In early 1943,

the *Panzertruppen* officially became a separate branch of the German army.

The German military invasion of Poland in September of 1939, was the culmination of 20 years of restructuring by the German army. Motorized formations of tanks and infantry, supported by artillery and aircraft, punched through the Polish lines of defense and encircled the enemy forces. The world was stunned. Not only had a new type of warfare begun, but other armies realized that their tactical doctrine lagged dangerously behind that of the German army. British and American journalists referred to this new warfare as "blitzkrieg" or "lightning war." The German army, on the other hand, saw it as a return to their traditional military operational concept of *Bewegungskrieg*, a war of maneuver and mobility.

Blitzkrieg was not a doctrine developed by just one person. Recently, author and historian Robert Citino called Germany "the test bed and birthplace of mechanized warfare." Other countries were developing similar mechanized forces on much more limited budgets and time scales. Germany was the first to demonstrate that it had a balance between doctrine and tactics in the form of combined-arms operations. Germany was fortunate to already have a long traditional doctrinal basis for maneuver and mobility in warfare dating back many decades. Blitzkrieg, then, can be viewed as the logical evolution of maneuver warfare, combining traditional concepts of warfare with technological advances into an operational concept of offensive, combined-arms warfare.

For the two years following the successful invasion and conquest of Poland, the German army's audacity, innovation, flexibility, fluid movements, and intense planning in their military operations—combining airborne and amphibious landings with concentrated panzer thrusts—swept aside all that stood in their path. However, not everything was what it seemed. Despite all the meticulous preparation made by German planners, serious problems would enter into all their operations. Some of these problems were the result of conservative operational planning and maintenance issues that would render entire *panzer divisions* combat ineffective. Added to the problems were horse-drawn infantry supply columns that clogged the path of armored assaults, interference in operations by both senior military and political leaders, and the inevitable confusion of war. The German army's *panzer divisions* were fit only for very short military campaigns against isolated opponents. They were not prepared for a protracted war of attrition, as occurred when the German army attempted to conquer the Soviet Union beginning in the summer of 1941.

Eventually, the Germans became unable to mobilize their economy and industry to support the war effort. After two years of war, when the German forces prepared to enter Russia, German industry started to fall short of meeting the increasing needs of the army. New divisions sent to the front had to make do with second-rate captured French military equipment. In 1940, for example, plans for expanding tank production were cancelled due to the cost and the lack of manpower availability. Realistic projections showed that German industrial capacity would not be in full swing until 1943. But, Hitler went ahead anyway and launched his war at least four years prematurely.

During the course of World War II, the number of *panzer divisions* within the German army rose to over 30. While the number of *panzer divisions* increased, the number of tanks per division was getting progressively smaller. A late-war *panzer division* with 100 operational tanks was a rarity.

PZ.KPFW. I AUSF. A: PROBLEMS

Most of the German army officers concerned with the design, development, and fielding of the Pz.Kpfw. I Ausf. A were realistic about the tank's battlefield effectiveness. As early as 1933, a German army officer wrote anonymously in a military magazine that the future Pz.Kpfw. I Ausf. A was so beset with design shortcomings that it was completely unsuitable for combat and was fit only for driving around in parades.

In 1936, Hitler ordered a number of Pz.Kpfw. I Ausf. A tanks to be sent to Spain, along with German army volunteers, to take part in the ongoing Spanish Civil War (1936–1939). Their debut in combat was not impressive. One observer noted that "the machine made a somewhat worn out, and by no means modern, impression. Its effect

This Pz.Kpfw. I Ausf. F. is a wonderful example of the German army wasting its time and money on a design dead end. Originally created as a heavily armored infantry-support tank, the F model was slow, heavy, over-designed, and under-armed. Only a small number came off the production line before those in charge realized the mistake they had made and cancelled the rest of the order. *Patton Museum*

PzKpfw I Ausf F
(VK 1801)
Infantry Support Tank

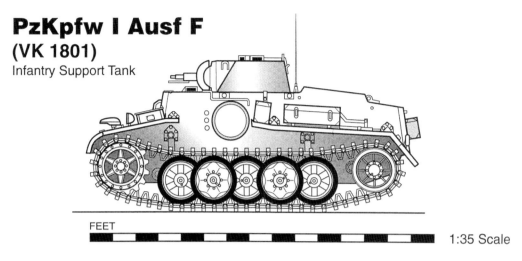

1:35 Scale

FEET

About 30 of these vehicles were produced
by Krauss-Maffei between mid 1940 and late 1942.

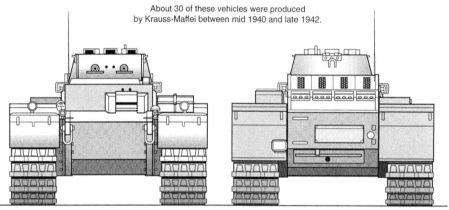

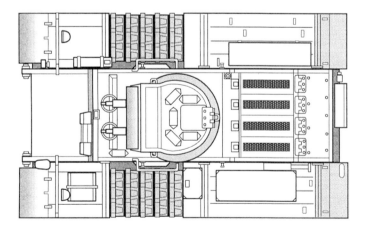

This line drawing shows a variety of views of the Pz.Kpfw. I Ausf. F. At least eight of these tanks were sent to Russia along with the 1st Panzer Division in early 1943. What results these vehicles achieved in the field are lost to history. Most remaining examples of the Pz.Kpfw. I Ausf. F saw use as training vehicles only. *George Bradford*

This column of Pz.Kpfw. II Ausf. A light tanks is crossing a bridge during the German military invasion of France in the summer of 1940. Prior to the introduction of the Ausf. A version of the Pz.Kpfw. II into German army service, the front transmission housing was rounded. With the introduction of the Pz.Kpfw. II Ausf. A into service, a new, better-armored, squared-off front transmission housing appeared. *Patton Museum*

is very slight, and it can hardly be considered a decisive weapon in local combat formations."

A major weakness of the Pz.Kpfw. I Ausf. A tanks deployed to Spain was their inferior firepower. Enemy tanks—like the Russian T26 light tanks and the BT-5 fast tank armed with 45mm high-velocity main guns—successfully engaged and destroyed the German light tanks long before they were within effective firing range. Even within range, the two turret-mounted machine guns of the Pz.Kpfw. I tank were useless against the steel armor of the T26 and BT-5. In an effort to even the odds between the German and Russian tanks fighting in Spain, some of the German tanks had a turret-mounted 20mm automatic cannon installed.

A column of German tanks advances into the Soviet Union in the summer of 1941. In the foreground is a Pz.Kpfw. II Ausf. C. Like it predecessors, it originally appeared in service with armor only 0.58 inch (14.5 millimeters) thick. Because combat experience showed this to be inadequate, in early 1940, most Pz.Kpfw. IIs had additional 0.8-inch-thick (20 millimeters) armor plates bolted on the front of the tank's turret, superstructure, and hull, as seen in this picture. *Patton Museum*

PzKpfw II Ausf C
Serving in North Africa c. 1941

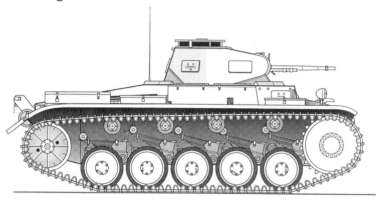

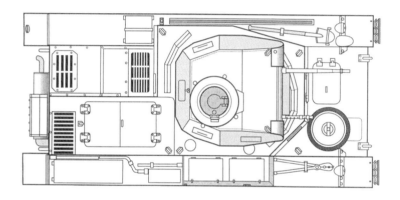

FEET
1:35 scale

0   5   10   15   20

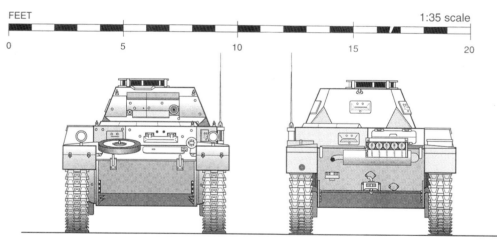

The A through F models of the Pz.Kpfw. II came with a simple split hatch for the vehicle commander in the roof of the vehicle's turret. In early 1940, the German army began replacing it with a circular tank commander's cupola containing eight periscopes and a single-hinged hatch cover, as visible in this line drawing of a Pz.Kpfw. II Ausf. C. This cupola became a standard production fixture in the Pz.Kpfw. II Ausf. F. The 20mm main gun in the manually rotated turret weighed 139 pounds (63 kilograms) and had a rate of fire of 280 rounds per minute. The weapon fed from a 10-round magazine, of which 18 could be stored in the tank. *George Bradford*

A FOLLOW-ON VERSION APPEARS

Because the Krupp engine in the Pz.Kpfw. I Ausf. A provided insufficient mobility, 100-horsepower, water-cooled, six-cylinder Maybach engines were installed beginning in 1935. Krupp also added an upgraded transmission to handle the extra power. A British army report from August 1941, contains impressions of German tank engines, reading, "Vehicles examined have proved to be very adequately powered. The power-to-weight ratio aimed at by the German tank designers when a new tank is put into production appears to be in the region of 16–20 horsepower per ton. All tanks so far examined are driven by petrol [gasoline] engines. It will be remembered that the Italian medium tanks M-11 and M-13 have diesel engines."

The larger size of the new Maybach liquid-cooled gasoline engine required an enlarged engine compartment. Accordingly, the Pz.Kpfw. I Ausf. A hull was lengthened. The longer hull then required an additional road wheel on either side. The redesigned hull also allowed for the addition of raised idler wheels at the rear; no longer did the idler wheels also have to serve as road wheels. The suspension changes reduced track-throwing incidents, and the longer wheelbase provided the vehicle with more stable handling and riding characteristics.

The raised idlers and longer wheelbase are the major external spotting features for this improved version of the Pz.Kpfw. I series, which was assigned the designation the Ausf. B. The weight of the larger vehicle was more than 6 tons (5.4 metric tons). It was 14 feet 6 inches (4.4 meters) long, 6 feet 9 inches (2.1 meters) wide and 5 feet 7.7 inches (1.7 meters) high.

The same four companies that built the Pz.Kpfw. I Ausf. A started producing the Ausf. B version in the late summer of 1935. Production continued until the summer of 1937, with 399 units delivered.

The lack of firepower and armor protection on the Pz.Kpfw. I series resulted in their withdrawal from frontline service by early 1941. However, some would remain in service as command-and-control vehicles until 1944. Many vehicles were modified into self-propelled artillery, turretless ammunition re-supply, and other mission roles.

Krauss-Maffei produced a small number of Pz.Kpfw. I Ausf. C and Pz.Kpfw. I Ausf. F vehicles in 1942. The Ausf. C was dramatically different from the A and B models. It featured a turret-mounted 20mm automatic cannon and a 7.92mm machine gun. It was also more thickly armored, with a maximum frontal armor thickness of 1.2 inches (30 millimeters), compared to 0.52 inch (13 millimeters) on the original Pz.Kpfw. I Ausf. A and B. The weight of the additional armor and the larger main gun pushed the vehicle's weight to more than 9 tons (8.2 metric tons), which required a more powerful water-cooled 150-horsepower Maybach gasoline engine. Top speed was 49 miles per hour (79 kilometers per hour) for the Pz.Kpfw. I Ausf. C. The Ausf. C also received a torsion bar suspension system utilizing an arrangement of large, overlapping road wheels. The wheels were large enough to support the return strand, so there was no need for track-support rollers. Only 40 Pz.Kpfw. I Ausf. Cs were produced.

On display at the Tank Museum in Bovington, United Kingdom, is this Pz.Kpfw. II Ausf. F featuring an early-war German army paint scheme. The vehicle commander in any of the various versions of the Pz.Kpfw. II-series tanks fired the 20mm main gun with a handle on the gun's elevating hand wheel. *Tank Museum–Bovington*

The Pz.Kpfw. I Ausf. F was a specialized version of the series intended only as a heavily-armored infantry support tank. The F version used the chassis and suspension system of the Pz.Kpfw. I Ausf. C. It boasted a maximum frontal armor thickness of 3.2-inches (80 millimeters) and a side armor thickness of 2 inches (50 millimeters). This impressive armor arrangement came at a heavy price; the vehicle weighted almost 20 tons (18 metric tons). Armament consisted of just two side-by-side 7.92mm turret-mounted machine guns. The German army soon realized that the time and effort put into the design and building of the Pz.Kpfw. I Ausf. F was a luxury that the German industry could ill afford, and that its great weight, slow speed, and light armament were going to make it ineffective as an infantry-support tank. Only 30 units were built.

A NEW LIGHT TANK: PANZERKAMPFWAGEN II

Even before the first production example of the Pz.Kpfw. I Ausf. A rolled off the assembly line, the German army was planning for a larger and better armed and armored light tank. That vehicle turned out to be Pz.Kpfw. II series. This new light tank received power from a water-cooled Maybach gasoline engine, as did all subsequent German tanks built during World War II.

Most tank development to this day starts with the construction of a number of prototype vehicles meant to identify and correct any design shortcomings before series production begins. The Germans built their prototype tanks for the Pz.Kpfw. II series between the summers of 1936 and 1937.

The first series production version was the Pz.Kpfw. II Ausf. A, which started production in July of 1937. It was 15 feet 9 inches (4.8 meters) long, with a width of 7 feet 6 inches (2.3 meters). The tank was a bit more than 7 feet (2.23 meters) tall, weighed about 8 tons (7.3 metric tons), and had a crew of three men. The driver and radio operator were seated in the hull, with the driver in the front of the hull and the radioman under the turret in a rear-facing seat. The vehicle commander sat on a seat suspended from the hand-operated turret. He aimed, fired, and loaded the vehicle's weapons, which consisted of a 20mm automatic cannon and a 7.92mm machine gun.

The official military designation of the main gun that appeared on all pilot and series production versions of the Pz.Kpfw. II was 2cm Kw.K. 30. The letters *Kw.K.* are a German abbreviation for *kampfwagenkanone,* or tank gun. The weapon was fed from a metal box (called a magazine by the military) that held 10 rounds. The 2cm Kw.K. could only be fired in full automatic mode. It was incapable of firing single shots.

A 1939 German army training manual describes the method of employment of the 2cm Kw.K. 30 mounted on the Pz.Kpfw. II: "Short bursts of two or three rounds is the normal method of engaging targets from fire positions or on the move." The manual goes on to talk about the choice of targets and their recommend combat ranges: "Enemy tanks should be engaged from static fire positions at a range of 600 meters [660 yards]. The gun can also be used against enemy antitank guns at ranges of 500 meters [550 yards], but only if it is impossible to outflank the enemy and engage it with machine guns."

American soldiers are taking a captured Pz.Kpfw. II Ausf. F out for a test drive somewhere in North Africa in early 1943. All of the tank's vision ports are open as well as the driver's lower front-hull access hatch. While the vehicle commander on the Pz.Kpfw. II aimed his turret-mounted weapons with the aid of a 2.5-power optical telescope, he could also aim them over open sights by looking through the open vision ports in the turret mantlet. *Tank Museum–Bovington*

The Panzerspähwagen II Luchs was developed for the German army as a full-tracked armored reconnaissance vehicle that would have excellent cross-country abilities, something badly lacking in the Pz.Kpfw. II series. The initial order called for 800 units, with the first 100 armed with a turret-mounted 20mm main gun and a 7.92mm machine gun fitted alongside. *Patton Museum*

There were numerous armor-protected vision ports in the turret and hull of Pz.Kpfw. II Ausf. A. The tank commander had an open sight for close targets and a 2.5-power optical sight for more distant targets. Communications between the vehicle commander and driver were through a voice tube.

Maximum frontal armor thickness on the first Pz.Kpfw. II Ausf. A was only 0.06 inch (15 millimeters). Combat experience from the German military invasion of Poland in September of 1939 had shown that the armor was easy penetrated by the Polish army's antitank guns. Starting in 1940, the frontal armor was upgraded with bolt-on armor plates of varying thicknesses.

The Pz.Kpfw. II Ausf. A, B, and C had five road wheels per side, isolated from the hull by leaf springs. Four track-return rollers supported the upper strand. Like all German army tanks, the Pz.Kpfw. II series had the transmission and drive sprockets in the front and the engine in the rear. Maximum speed of the Ausf. A, B, and C versions was 25 miles per hour (40 kilometers per hour). On a full load of fuel, the maximum effective range of the tanks was about 125 miles (200 kilometers). A variety of German firms built more than 1,000 units of the Pz.Kpfw. II Ausf. A, B, and C variants between early 1937 and early 1940.

Between early 1938 and late 1939, the German army built 50 Pz.Kpfw. II Ausf. D and E versions. The torsion bar suspension with large road wheels was a major mobility upgrade that eliminated the need for track return rollers. The manual transmission was replaced by an automatic transmission. The maximum speed of the Pz.Kpfw. II Ausf. D and E was 34 miles per hour (55 kilometers per hour).

The final production version of the Pz.Kpfw. II series based on the original Ausf. A design was the Ausf. F, of which FAMO built 524 units between early 1941 and December 1942. Its flat, box-like lower front hull made it visually different from the Ausf. A, B, and C versions. The lower front hulls of the earlier versions were more rounded in shape. The Pz.Kpfw. II Ausf. F featured a frontal armor thickness of 1.4 inches (35 millimeters) and eliminated the need for the bolt-on armor plates of the earlier models.

Following the Ausf. F, several other tanks bore the Pz.Kpfw. II designation, although they differed significantly in appearance from the Ausf. A-F series. The last of these variants was the Pz.Kpfw. II Ausf. L (Sd. Kfz. 123), named the *Luchs* (Lynx), also known as the Panzerspähwagen II (abbreviated Pz.Sp.Wg. II). MAN built about 100 units between late 1943 and early 1944. The Lynx was designed for a high-speed reconnaissance role and featured a torsion bar suspension system with large, overlapping road wheels. The tank also featured a turret-mounted 20mm automatic cannon (the 2cm Kw.K. 38) and a 7.92mm MG34. Follow-on vehicles were to have a 50mm main gun. Since production was cancelled after the first 100 were built, the up-armed version was never produced. Top speed of the *Luchs* was 37.7 miles per hour (60 kilometers per hour). The tank's larger hull and turret allowed for a four-man crew.

LIGHT-TANK TACTICS

A May 1943 Allied intelligence bulletin contained this description of the employment of the Pz.Kpfw. II light tank in North Africa:

> In German tank organizations, a light tank platoon consisting of seven Pz.Kw. 2s is an organic part both of the regimental headquarters company and the battalion headquarters company. The regimental light tank platoon is normally used for reconnaissance purposes. German doctrine covering the reconnaissance duties of patrols drawn from these platoons is summarized below. (It assumes that superior German forces are conducting an advance.)
>
> Teamwork, the Germans point out, is the secret of successful reconnaissance. They believe that haphazardly formed reconnaissance patrols, made up of men who have never worked together before, are of little value.
>
> It is prohibited to take written orders and situation maps on reconnaissance. Special precautions are insisted upon when markings of any kind are made on maps used on reconnaissance; these markings are required to be of a kind which will not reveal German dispositions if the maps are captured.
>
> *Information Needed Beforehand.* For its disposition and method of work, the German patrol depends on knowing [the following]: Up to what point contact with the opposition is unlikely. (Until reaching this point, the patrol saves time by advancing rapidly and avoiding elaborate protective measures.) At what point contact is probable. (After this, increased alertness is maintained). At what point contact is certain. (Here the patrol is ready for action.)
>
> The patrol commander is also given necessary particulars regarding air support and information as to the attitude of the civil population.
>
> The light tank patrol advances rapidly from one observation point to the next, making use at first of roads and paths, but later, as it approaches hostile forces, using all available cover. When approaching villages, woods, or defiles, the patrol leaves the road in sufficient time to upset the opposition's aimed antitank-fire calculations.
>
> The German patrol commander makes a rapid estimate of our position and tries to attack and overrun us if he thinks that we are weak. If such a move does not seem advisable, he attempts to discover the type and strength of the opposition encountered, without becoming involved in combat.

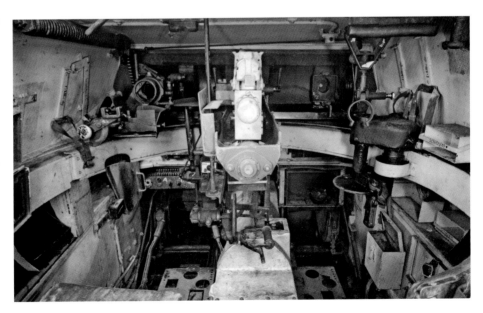

This picture shows the interior of the front of the turret and hull from a Panzerspähwagen II Luchs. Visible are the breech end of the 20mm main gun in the center of the turret and the mounting bracket for the 7.92mm machine gun not fitted in this vehicle, on the left. The bracket for fitting the vehicle's optical sight is on the right side of the main gun. *Patton Museum*

Panzerspähwagen II (2cm) "Luchs" (Sd.Kfz.123)

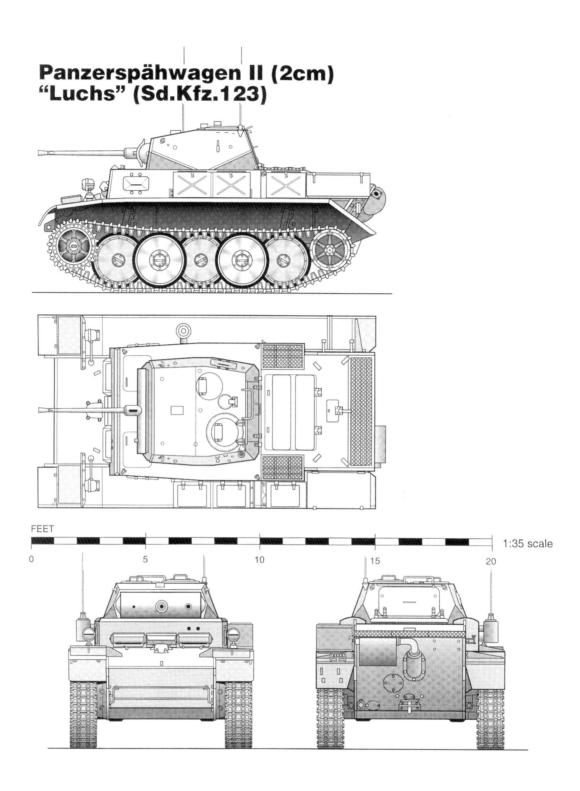

FEET

0   5   10   15   20

1:35 scale

The original plans for the Panzerspähwagen II Luchs called for all production units after the 100th vehicle to come with a turret mounting both a 50mm main gun and a 7.92mm machine gun. Because the first 100 production units of the Luchs proved unreliable in field use, the German army cancelled the remaining order for 700 up-gunned vehicles.

George Bradford

"Keen, capable, and well-trained officers or noncoms must be selected to command the light tank patrol," the Germans state. "These must be constituted of quick-thinking, resourceful troops who have functioned as a unit long enough to know and have confidence in their leader."

The mission of reconnaissance after H-hour is to explore the hostile position in detail, to protect German deployment, and to discover hostile gun positions, as well as natural and artificial obstacles in the line of advance.

The mission is carried out by light tank patrols (which may be reinforced) operating ahead or on the flanks, as in reconnaissance before H-hour. The reconnaissance tanks employed immediately ahead or to a forward flank are detailed automatically by the first wave of the attacking force. (Normally, [this includes] one light tank per platoon of heavier tanks in the first wave, and always the same light tank. The remaining light tanks work behind the first wave, performing other duties.) The reconnaissance tanks advance rapidly, making for suitable high ground. They keep 300 to 500 yards ahead of the first wave, and maintain visual contact with it. The reconnaissance tanks observe from open turrets or, if fired on, through their telescopes, with turrets closed. They advance by bounds, from cover to cover, keeping the terrain ahead under continuous observation.

The tanks in the first wave, especially the Pz. Kw. 4s, cover the reconnaissance tanks as they advance.

When the reconnaissance tanks contact our infantry, they attempt to overrun us and, if they are successful, they report and continue their mission. A reconnaissance tank discovering hostile antitank weapons and artillery reports them, takes up a position, and waits for the rest of its company. While waiting, it fires on hostile antitank weapons.

Tanks are avoided, but are observed from concealed positions. The reconnaissance tanks report suitable terrain for meeting an attack by hostile tanks. As under the circumstances described in the previous paragraph, each reconnaissance tank waits for the rest of its company.

Opposition which begins to retreat is promptly attacked, the reconnaissance tanks reporting the development and continuing the pursuit.

In the event of an attack by the opposition, the reconnaissance tanks take up a position, meet the attack, report, and wait for the rest of their companies to come up.

In all these instances, the reconnaissance tanks avoid obstructing the field of fire of the heavier tanks following them. Throughout, the light tanks report by radio if it is available, by prearranged flag or smoke signals, or by significant firing or maneuvering.

A Russian tank encountered by the Pz.Kpfw. I Ausf. A light tank crews during the Spanish Civil War was the BT-5 Fast Tank. It featured a turret-mounted 45mm cannon and a 7.62mm machine gun. The top speed of the tank when running on tracks was 40 miles per hour (65 kilometers per hour). The Pz.Kpfw. I Ausf. A had a maximum speed of only 23 miles per hour (37.5 kilometers per hour). *Patton Museum*

Driving through a burning French town is a German army Pz.Kpfw. III Ausf. F, armed with a 37mm main gun. The Ausf. F was the second production version of the Pz.Kpfw. III tank series. Like all tanks in the Pz.Kpfw. III series, it had a crew of five men, with the tank commander, gunner, and loader in the turret, while the driver and radioman sat in the front hull. *Tank Museum–Bovington*

Pictured during a rare public demonstration arranged by the German Tank Museum is this nicely restored Pz.Kpfw. IV Ausf. G. It appears with the paint scheme and markings of a tank in North Africa between 1941 and 1943. *Thomas Anderson*

CHAPTER TWO

MEDIUM TANKS

ON JANUARY 11, 1934, the German army ordnance department held an important meeting to select the major pieces of hardware for use by the future panzer divisions. The group decided on two separate medium tank designs, each fulfilling a different mission role.

The smaller and lighter of the two medium tanks originally weighed about 15 tons (13.05 metric tons) and evolved into the Pz.Kpfw. III series beginning in 1936. The first version in the series was designated the Pz.Kpfw. III Ausf. A. Daimler-Benz was the manufacturer.

Befitting its intended role as a tank killer, the Pz.Kpfw. III Ausf. A appeared with a turret-mounted 37mm high-velocity main gun officially designated by the German army as the 3.7cm Kw.K. L/45. The designation L/45 represents a method of weapon classification employed by the German military before and during World War II to describe a weapon's length in relation to its caliber (bore diameter). The Kw.K. L/45 gun barrel was 45 times the 37mm bore diameter, or 166.5 centimeters long. In English units, this is 5.47 feet.

In current American military terminology, the main gun ammunition used by all German tanks in World War II was "fixed," meaning that the metal cartridge case containing the primer and propelling charge was attached to the projectile. The fixed round was loaded into the gun as a single unit, with the projectile being that part of the round that the propellant fires from the barrel.

The 37mm main gun on the Pz.Kpfw. III Ausf. A fired armor-piercing (AP) and high-explosive (HE) ammunition. An AP round is referred to in German as *Panzergranate* or *PzGr*. The HE round was designed for use against enemy infantry and towed antitank guns. In German, high-explosive rounds are *Sprenggranate*, or just *SprGr*. All German tank main-gun rounds came with a tracer element to allow the crew to observe the trajectory (flight path) of their shots as they headed toward their chosen targets.

AP rounds are also referred to as kinetic energy (KE) projectiles, which cause damage by transferring their kinetic energy (toughness and striking velocity) to targets. The hardness and shape of the KE projectile also contributes to target damage. As range increases, KE projectiles slow down due to air resistance. There is also a trajectory effect. At longer ranges, the trajectory is curved,

PzKpfw III Ausf F (1939)
with 3.7cm KwK L46.5
(SdKfz 141)

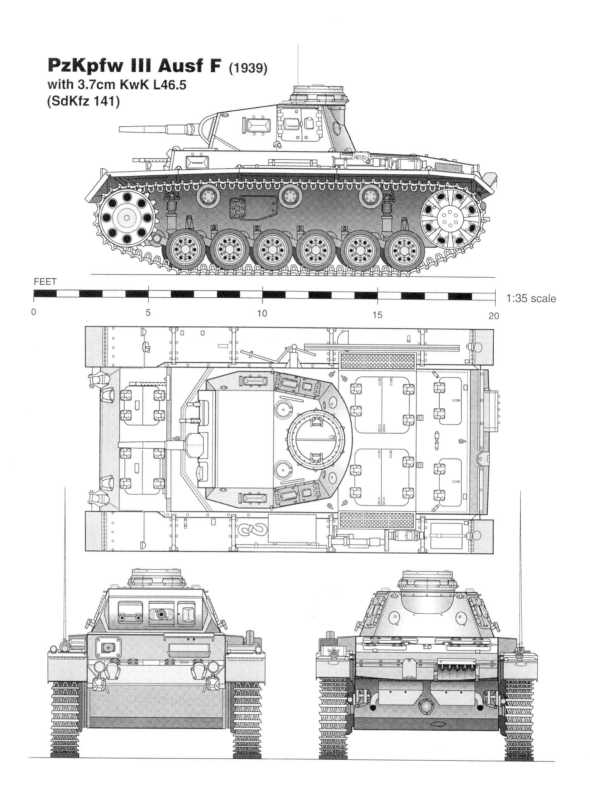

FEET

0   5   10   15   20

1:35 scale

This four-view line drawing shows the various external features of the Pz.Kpfw. III Ausf. F armed with the 37mm main gun. The driver and radioman in the front hull of all Pz.Kpfw. III-series tanks did not have the overhead armored hatches seen on other German medium and heavy tanks. Instead, they entered and exited the vehicle by way of hatches on either side of the vehicle's lower hull. *George Bradford*

so the projectile impacts on a target at an angle to the horizontal.

The 37mm KE projectile fired from the Pz.Kpfw. III Ausf. A main gun was a solid slug of high-hardness steel. This type of projectile is categorized as an "inert" projectile, since it contains no explosive element. In World War II, inert projectiles with no internal cavity went by the name "shot" in the American and British armies. A projectile with an internal cavity, capable of containing such things as HE or smoke, was generally referred to as a "shell" or "filled."

At ranges shorter than about 500 yards (457 meters), the Pz.Kpfw. III Ausf. A KE projectile could penetrate 2.8 inches (70 millimeters) of steel armor sloped at 30 degrees. At 1,000 yards (914 meters), this dropped to just a little more than 1 inch (31 millimeters) of steel armor sloped at 30 degrees. Targets exceeding 2,000 yards (1,828 meters) were beyond the gun's range.

Range-related terms are broken down into a couple of different categories. The term "maximum range" means the longest distance a projectile can go, regardless of terminal effect. For direct-fire weapons, like tank main guns, this is usually only of interest to the people who have to draw firing-range safety fans. The term "maximum effective range" is determined by the ability to get the projectile to hit the target, and the ability of the projectile to penetrate the target, given a hit.

When the gunner pulled the trigger in the Pz.Kpfw. III Ausf. A, an electrical current traveled through the breechblock into the primer element located within the cartridge case. The primer produced a small explosion that ignited the much larger propelling charge contained within the cartridge case. As the propelling charge burned within the cartridge case, it produced a large quantity of gas under great pressure between the breechblock and the projectile. Because the gaseous energy follows the path of least resistance, the projectile moved forward in response, accelerating rapidly as it traveled down the gun tube. Soft metal bands, called rotating or driving bands, at the rear of the projectile imparted rifling torque by engaging the spiral grooves (rifling) along the length of the gun tube. Rifling was standard on all German tank guns of World War II. Rotation of a projectile produces a more stable flight trajectory due to gyroscopic effects. The rotating bands also helped to minimize leakage of the gases pushing the projectile down the gun tube.

In addition to the 37mm main gun, the Pz.Kpfw. III Ausf. A also carried three 7.92mm machine guns. Two were coaxial and followed the aim of the main gun. The third was operated by the radioman in the front of the vehicle. Armor protection on the five-man, gasoline-powered tank was a maximum of 0.6 inch (15 millimeters) on the turret, hull, and superstructure.

The German invasion of France in the summer of 1940 demonstrated to the German army that the Pz.Kpfw. III was both under-gunned and under-armored. To correct these design shortcomings, the Germans up-gunned the Pz.Kpfw. III series with a larger and more powerful 50mm main gun. They also began adding extra armor to the tanks. Both of these features appear on the Pz.Kpfw. III Ausf. F shown here on display at the Patton Museum of Cavalry and Armor. *Michael Green*

Three German army Pz.Kpfw. III-series tanks are using a railroad line as a road. The casual posture of the crews would indicate that enemy opposition is not expected. In the foreground is an updated Pz.Kpfw. III Ausf. G featuring a 50mm main gun. Both of the following tanks are in the original configuration of the Pz.Kpfw. III Ausf. F and feature 37mm main guns. *Tank Museum–Bovington*

DESIGN ISSUES

The selection of the 37mm main gun by the German army ordnance department for the Pz.Kpfw. III Ausf. A was made despite the strong objections of some senior panzer officers, who insisted that a 50mm high-velocity main gun was the minimum required to penetrate the armor on the newest generation of French, British, and Soviet tanks already in service. The final compromise agreement made the turret ring large enough to accept the mounting of a larger main gun if events dictated that it was needed.

The thorniest problem faced by Daimler-Benz in the design of the Pz.Kpfw. III Ausf. A was the development of a satisfactory suspension system. The German army disliked the original Ausf. A suspension system, which consisted of five large road wheels on each side isolated from the ground by coil springs. Small numbers of trial versions (Ausf. B through Ausf. D) featured a slightly different arrangement of eight smaller road wheels riding on leaf springs, as well as other minor changes.

The Ausf. B, C, and D versions of the Pz.Kpfw. III all took part in the German invasion of Poland in September 1939. However, due to their unsatisfactory suspension systems and other design issues, all were withdrawn from service before the German invasion of France and the Low Countries (Holland and Belgium) in the summer of 1940.

SERIES PRODUCTION BEGINS

It took the replacement of the coil springs with a torsion bar suspension system on the 19-ton (17.2 metric ton)

Ausf. E version before the German army ordnance office was satisfied enough with the performance to order series production to begin. Twelve transversely mounted high-hardness steel torsion bars connected to six road-arm stations on either side of the vehicle. The bars ran across the vehicle at floor level and connected to fixed anchors in the hull. Spindles fitted to the lower ends of the road-wheel arms accepted a pair of road wheels for each arm. There were 24 small road wheels on the Pz.Kpfw. III.

In order to speed up production, the Pz.Kpfw. III Ausf. E was built in multiple German factories. Ninety-six vehicles rolled of the assembly lines between late 1938 and late 1939. The tank itself was 17.6 feet (5.38 meters) long and 8 feet (2.44 meters) tall, with a width of 9.5 feet (2.91 meters). The tank's transmission provided the driver with 10 forward speeds and 4 in reverse. Maximum speed topped out at 24.5 miles per hour (40 kilometers per hour) on a level paved surface, while the maximum operational range was 102.5 miles (165 kilometers).

Combat experience in Poland quickly showed that the 0.6-inch-thick (15 millimeters) steel armor plate on the Ausf. B through D versions was too thin to stop penetration by enemy antitank guns. The Ausf. E version of the Pz.Kpfw. III featured 1.2-inch-thick (30 millimeters) steel armor plates on its turret, hull, and superstructure. The thicker steel armor on the Pz.Kpfw. III Ausf. E pushed its weight up to about 21 tons (19.05 metric tons). This extra weight also required the fitting of a more powerful 300-horsepower Maybach gasoline engine. Earlier versions of the tank featured a Maybach gasoline engine that had produced only 250 horsepower.

The Pz.Kpfw. III Ausf. E was followed by a number of progressively improved versions beginning with the Ausf. F., which differed only slightly from the Ausf. E. The only external difference between the two tanks was the addition of two small cast steel ventilation ducts for the brakes and final drives on the upper front hull plate of the Ausf. F version of the Pz.Kpfw. III.

Five factories produced 435 units of the Pz.Kpfw. III Ausf. F between late 1939 and the summer of 1940. The Pz.Kpfw. III Ausf. E and F made up the bulk of the medium tank fleet employed by the German army in the invasion of France in the summer of 1940.

The follow-on to the Ausf. F version of the Pz.Kpfw. III was the Ausf. G, of which 600 came off the assembly lines between early 1940 and early 1941. While the Ausf. G looked very similar to its predecessors, the Ausf. E and F, it featured an improved commander's cupola and a fold-down armored visor for the driver's direct-vision slit in the vehicle's front superstructure plate. Some of the German army's inventory of Pz.Kpfw. III Ausf. Gs took part in the German military invasion of France.

The Ausf. G version of the Pz.Kpfw. III had 1.2-inch-thick (30 millimeters) steel armor plates added to its existing 1.2-inch armor, giving it 2.4 inches (60 millimeters) of frontal armor protection. The add-on armor plates were later retrofitted to the older Ausf. E and F tanks.

The Pz.Kpfw. III Ausf. J, introduced in March of 1941, started out with 2 inches (50 millimeters) of steel frontal armor on the gun turret mantlet (gun shield), hull, and superstructure. By the following month, however, they added 0.8 inch (20 millimeters) of spaced armor plate to the turret mantlet and the front superstructure of the vehicle.

A British army report dated October 5, 1941 discusses the German Army's fondness for adding extra armor to their tanks:

The thickness of armour on the German tanks will be seen to be in excess of what was originally thought. It has been recognized ever since the Germans tried their tanks out in Spain (Spanish Civil War) that they were striving to increase the armour protection of their vehicles, but one was reluctant, knowing the Germans and their thorough

Forming part of the collection of the Patton Museum of Cavalry and Armor at Fort Knox, Kentucky, is this Pz.Kpfw. III Ausf. F. It is armed with the long-tube version of the 50mm main gun that upgraded many early-production Pz.Kpfw. III series when they were returned to various factories for rebuilding. *Dean and Nancy Kleffman*

PzKpfw III Ausf L
(SdKfz 141/1)

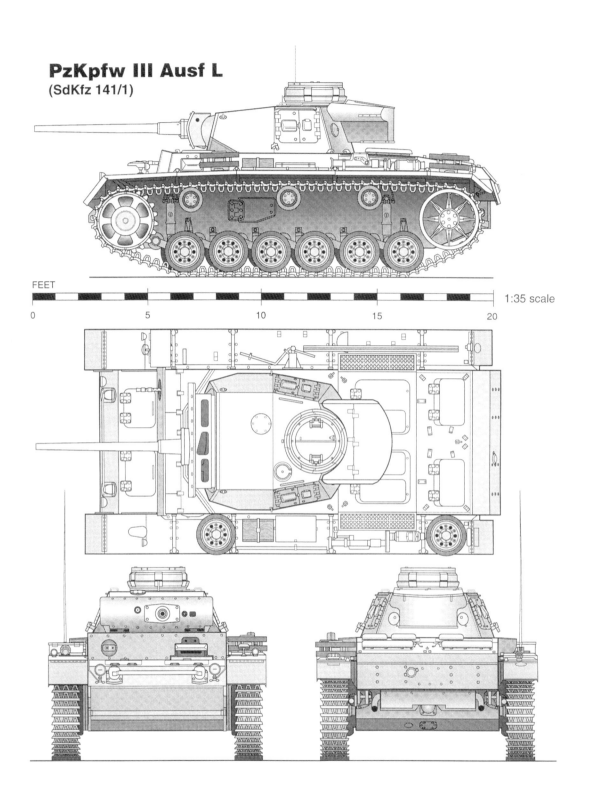

FEET

0   5   10   15   20

1:35 scale

In this four-view line drawing of a Pz.Kpfw. III Ausf. L, the various external features of the tank are clearly seen. Instead of an overhead periscope, the driver on all Pz.Kpfw. III-series tanks had a direct-vision port located in the front superstructure glacis plate, which was protected by a hinged armored flap that could open and close from within the vehicle. *George Bradford*

This restored Pz.Kpfw. III Ausf. L tank belongs to the very large collection of the Tank Museum in Bovington, United Kingdom, which exceeds over 300 vehicles. The pronounced overhang of the main gun over the front of this vehicle shows it to be armed with the long-tube version of the 50mm main gun. Roughly half the original order for the Ausf. L version of the Pz.Kpfw. III came off the production lines armed with a low-velocity short-tube 75mm main gun. *Tank Museum–Bovington*

methods, to believe that they had gone to such lengths of improvisation as now seem evident.

All armour plating is welded with a half-V welding. This method of construction does not enable the plates to stand up to very heavy punishment, and there is a marked tendency to crack along the joints. The quality of armor plate appears to be definitely inferior to that which the Czechs produced for instance . . . . Instead of redesigning their tanks straight away when they discovered that the armour protection was inadequate, the Germans have overcome their difficulties by welding or bolting supplementary plates of armour on those places, which by experience they have discovered are the most vulnerable spots. In this way their tank production has not been interfered with.

A NEW MAIN GUN APPEARS

Combat experience had demonstrated that the senior panzer leaders were correct about the inadequacy of the Pz.Kpfw. III's 37mm main gun. In response, a new 50mm main gun designated the 5cm Kw.K. L/42 soon appeared on the Ausf. H in October of 1940. By April of 1941, 308 Pz.Kpfw. III Ausf. H tanks had come out of the factories.

The new 6.89-foot-long (2.1 meters), 50mm main gun also began appearing on the Pz.Kpfw. III Ausf. G during production beginning in October of 1940. The German army then retrofitted the previous-production Ausf. G, E, and F versions with the 50mm main gun as quickly as they could. The Pz.Kpfw. III Ausf. G was the first version to dispense with the second coaxial 7.92mm machine gun in the turret.

The new 50mm main gun mounted on the Pz.Kpfw. III could fire a wider range of rounds than the original 37mm main gun. Combat experience had shown that the conventional blunt-nosed steel AP round would shatter on impact with newer types of face-hardened steel armor plate. Face-hardened armor plate is normal steel armor plate put through an extra heating process to harden its outer surface, while retaining the toughness of the original armor plate.

The German solution was the armor-piercing capped (APC) round. This round has a strong penetrative cap fitted over the blunt nose of a standard steel AP round, which reduced its tendency to shatter on contact with hardened armor. The cap also assisted in turning the projectile into the sloping armor of an enemy tank, thus improving the odds of penetration.

A third type of AP round was the armor-piercing, composite rigid (APCR) round. APCR rounds consist of a sub-caliber tungsten core centered within a lightweight

Pictured during a public demonstration hosted by the Deutsches Panzermuseum (German Tank Museum), Munster, Germany, is a nicely restored and running Pz.Kpfw. III Ausf. M. One of the external spotting features for this version of the Pz.Kpfw. III is the absence of the crew ingress and egress hatches located on either side of the vehicle's hull. *Thomas Anderson*

metal carrier that travels to the target along with the sub-caliber core. Upon impact, the lightweight metal carrier strips away from the very dense and hard sub-caliber core, which continues on to penetrate the armor. In addition to the AP rounds, the 50mm main gun on the up-gunned Pz.Kpfw III also fired a conventional HE round against enemy infantry, towed antitank guns, and other lightly armored targets.

The introduction of a larger main gun on the Pz.Kpfw III was not a surprise to the British army, as is seen in this extract from a report dated October 5, 1941: "The mounting of the 50mm Q.F. (quick-firing) gun in the Pz.Kw. III is the only innovation encountered in the armament. This has been expected for some time by the British General Staff, as the original 37mm gun has not proved sufficiently effective against British A.F.V.s (armored fighting vehicles) in France (summer 1940)."

HITLER GETS INVOLVED

The fitting of the 50mm main gun designated 5cm Kw.K. L/42 into the Pz.Kpfw. III took place against Hitler's wishes. In February of 1941, he had ordered that all Pz.Kpfw. IIIs come armed with the 5cm Kw.K. 39 L/60 guns, a longer and more powerful 50mm main gun with a length of 9.85 feet (3 meters). The German army ordnance

department ignored this order, due to supply difficulties in obtaining the longer 50mm main gun and the department's belief that the existing shorter 50mm main gun was potent enough to deal with any battlefield opponents. This assumption was disproved during the German invasion of the Soviet Union in the summer of 1941. The Red Army's T34/76 medium tank and their KV-series heavy tanks were immune to penetration by the original 50mm main gun mounted on the Pz.Kpfw. IIIs.

Upon learning that the German army ordnance office had disregarded his wishes, Hitler demanded that the longer 50mm main gun be introduced halfway through the production order for the Ausf. J version of the Pz.Kpfw. III. The longer 50mm main-gun barrel first appeared in December 1941. All earlier-version Pz.Kpfw. III-series tanks that returned to Germany from the battlefields were retrofitted with the longer 50mm main gun. Almost 2,000 Pz.Kpfw. III-series medium tanks fitted with the more lethal 50mm main gun came out of the factories between the end of 1941 and the first few months of 1943.

It is worth noting that it was normal practice for many German tanks to have features of more than one variant, as depot rebuilds added compatible features from later-production batches. Guns, sprockets, idlers, bolt-on armor, and various other bits and pieces were often mixed and matched, making positive identification of tanks in historical photographs extremely difficult.

VEHICLE DESCRIPTION

The major combatants of World War II strove to collect information on any piece of military equipment employed by their opponents. The introduction of a new tank was always of great interest. Occasionally, technical evaluations took place under enemy observation. A British army report dated July 21, 1942, contains this colorful description by a British army officer seeking technical information about a destroyed and abandoned German army Pz.Kpfw. III with the long 50mm main gun, called the "Mark III special" by the British army:

In the first place, the Mark 3 "special" was knocked out in the central sector in an area which remained on the warm side for quite a considerable period. The whole setup in fact was distinctly unpromising. Apart from all this, the enemy was sitting practically on top of it, and fully realizing that it was there, he appeared to resent most strongly my interest. An examination carried out mainly on one's tummy, with one eye permanently and furtively looking over the left shoulder, and with the hand not using the pencil holding a trembling pistol, is not an ideal way of reporting on the techni-

cal data of a new tank. This accounts for the scrappy and rather disjointed report which I was able to send back, since I was not on any occasion allowed there long and several times prevented from getting there at all, one unfortunate man being apparently regarded as a fit target for artillery fire—a thoroughly unsporting attitude.

The tank was a normal Mark 3 Model J (there was no I model), or J, with a 50mm armour basis . . . apart from the gun and the extra spaced armour, I could find no new features whatsoever. Since, however, the tank was in a very bad shape, the inside of the hull and turret being burnt out and full of half burnt Germans, it would not be possible for me to say that there were in fact no other changes of design. I particularly tried to find out what had happened to the ammunition stowage, but it was quite impossible to tell. There was only one cartridge case left intact and this I recovered and brought back.

On my first visit to the tank, the gun, with the various odd bits and pieces belonging to it, was half buried, and I had to dig it out. The result was that everything was thickly covered with sand. On close examination it is confirmed that the chamber and

A rear view of a Pz.Kpfw. III Ausf. M belonging to the German Tank Museum. This was the last Pz.Kpfw. III-series tank armed with a 50mm main gun. By the time it starting coming off of the production lines in late 1942, it was clear the vehicle had no future as a medium tank, being under-gunned and under-armored. The initial order for 1,000 units of the tank was later cut to only 250 units. *Thomas Anderson*

This picture shows a privately-owned Pz.Kpfw. III tank armed with the long-tube version of the 50mm main gun. It has the hull of an Ausf. M or later N version (as evident by the lack of the hull side hatches) and the smoke grenade launchers of the turret of the Ausf. M or N. However, the turret has the vision ports from an earlier version, such as an Ausf. J or early-production Ausf. L version of the Pz.Kpfw. III. *Bob Fleming/Panzer Prints*

interior of the bore is exactly the same, or very nearly so, as the Pak 38 (towed antitank gun). The overall length from the breach opening to the muzzle proved on measurement, to be 9 feet 4 inches (279 centimeters). It seems obvious that the gun is not intended to take a muzzle brake, and the piece has been designed for a recoil into a cylindrical cradle instead of the normal Pak 38 type.

A more detailed general description of a Pz.Kpfw. III Ausf. E, F, or G version appeared in an Allied informational booklet released in October of 1944:

The PzKpfw III is a tank of the cruiser class. The weight is about 22 tons (19.8 metric tons), and its armament now consists of a long-barreled 5cm gun (5cm Kw.K. L/60) with a coaxial MG (machine gun) mounted in the turret and one hull MG mounted on the right-hand side of the front superstructure. In addition, small arms are carried, such as machine carbines, egg grenades, (and) a signal pistol, besides each member of the crew being armed with a revolver.

The tank is divided from front to rear into three separate compartments. At the front is the driver's

On display at the Tank Museum–Bovington is this cut-away example of a Pz.Kpfw. III Ausf. N, the last production version of the tank. Rather than being armed with a 50mm main gun, which was no longer able to penetrate the armor of Red Army tanks, the German army decided to mount a short-tube, low-velocity 75mm main gun in the tank, inherited from the early version of the Pz.Kpfw. IV medium tank. *Tank Museum–Bovington*

compartment; he sits on the left hand side with his steering levers and foot controls immediately in front of him. The gearbox (transmission) (above which is the instrument board) and the gear lever is on his right and a parking brake on his left. The steering mechanism is either hydraulically or mechanically operated and is of the epicyclic brake type. He has a vision port, protected by a laminated glass block and an outer armoured visor, to look through forwards. When the visor is closed, the driver slides an episcope into position—two holes are drilled through the front superstructure plate above the visor for this purpose. When the ordinary vision port is in use, these two apertures are covered by a plate on the inside. There is another port behind the driver's left shoulder; it is fitted with a readily removable glass block.

The wireless (radio) operator sits next to the driver on the right-hand side of the tank. He has a hull MG in a ball mounting which is controlled by a headrest attached to the mounting. The brow pad and telescope eyepiece are all fixed on the same mounting so that as he moves his head to direct the MG, his eye is always in the centre of his sight. The wireless equipment is normally situated to the left of the operator, over the gearbox, although sometimes a small set may be found in front of him under the glacis plate. There is a revolver port by

Taking part in the invasion of Poland in September 1939, is this Pz.Kpfw. IV Ausf. A. The relaxed and cheerful expressions on the crew members' faces seem to indicate that victory was at hand. Only 35 units of the Ausf. A version of the Pz.Kpfw. IV series rolled off the factory floor between late 1937 and early 1938 before an improved version entered into production.
Patton Museum

his right shoulder inset into the right side of the superstructure. Neither the driver nor the wireless operator have access hatches in the top of the superstructure.

The fighting compartment surmounted by the turret is in the centre. On the PzKpfw III, there is no floor in the turret, although seats for the commander and gunner are suspended from the turret

Beginning in April 1938, production of an Ausf. B version of the Pz.Kpfw. IV series began. While it looked very similar to the Pz.Kpfw. IV Ausf. A, there were a number of improvements to the vehicle. Besides a new type of tank commander's cupola, the vehicle came with a new, more powerful engine and a six-speed transmission, in contrast to the five-speed transmission in the Pz.Kpfw. IV Ausf. A. *Patton Museum*

A German army Pz.Kpfw. IV Ausf. C is rolling through an occupied Polish town in late September 1939. It came with a redesigned mantlet and modified engine mounts. One of the most noticeable external differences between this tank and its direct predecessor, the Pz.Kpfw. IV Ausf. B, was the deletion of the machine gun mount in the front hull and its replacement with a simple observation flap for the radioman.
Patton Museum

wall. *The loader, who stands on the right-hand side of the gun, has no seat and must therefore walk around with the turret as it traverses (starting with the Ausf. H a turret basket appeared on the PzKpfw III). He has a vision port protected by a glass block and an outer flap on the right-hand side of the turret. The gunner sits forward on the left-hand side of the gun. The 5cm gun is fired electrically by means of a trigger on the turret traverse hand-wheel, and the coaxial MG mechanically by a foot-operated trigger. A vision port similar to the loader's is provided on the left-hand side of the turret. The commander sits in the middle at the rear of the turret, directly behind the main armament. His cupola is integral with the turret, and six ports fitted with bulletproof glass blocks and sliding steel shutters provide all-round vision. The cupola hatch consists of two hinged flaps. An auxiliary turret-traversing handle on the loader's side allows dual control for quick traversing, as no power traverse is provided on this tank.*

The engine compartment is at the rear and is separated from the fighting compartment by a bulkhead. The engine is mounted in the centre with a petrol tank and a battery box on either side. To the rear of the engine are situated two radiators lying across the tank. A cardan (universal joint) shaft runs to the front of the tank under the 'dummy' floor of the fighting compartment. There is an escape hatch on either side of the hull in line with the fighting compartment.

The normal target and turret position indicating devices are provided for the commander and gunner, respectively, and a gyroscopic compass (Kurskreisel) is fitted for the driver.

THE FINAL PRODUCTION VERSIONS

Following the Pz.Kpfw. III Ausf. J into production was the very similar Ausf. L. The Ausf. J and L both featured the same long 50mm main gun. Between June and December 1942, 653 units of the Pz.Kpfw. IV Ausf. L were produced in multiple German factories. The last version of the Pz.Kpfw. III series armed with the long 50mm main gun was the roughly 22-ton (19.8 metric ton) Ausf. M, of which 250 units came off the assembly lines between late of 1942 and early 1943.

By then, it had become apparent to the German tank development community that the days of the Pz.Kpfw. III as a frontline tank had ended. To extend the useful service life of the Pz.Kpfw. III series, the German army ordnance department had considered mounting the turret of the Pz.Kpfw. IV tank, with its long-barreled 75mm main gun, on the chassis. The idea proved unworkable because the Pz.Kpfw. IV turret with its main gun was too heavy for the Pz.Kpfw. III chassis to carry. Fitting a larger 75mm main gun with a long gun tube into the Pz.Kpfw. III turret was not an option because the turret was too small.

Despite the obsolescence of the Pz.Kpfw. III series, the German army needed every tank it could possibly field. As a last resort, the army mounted in the turret of the Pz.Kpfw. III a short, 5.9-foot (1.80-cm) low-velocity 75mm tank gun designated the 7.5cm Kw.K. L/24. Tests showed that this was a workable solution, and the up-gunned Pz.Kpfw. III was designated the Ausf. N. This newly-fitted main gun fired a variety of main gun rounds, including an HE known as a high-explosive antitank (HEAT) round. In German military terminology, HEAT rounds are shaped-charge rounds, which translates in German to *hohlgranate*, *hohlraumgranate*, or *hohlraummunition*. The German military abbreviation for shaped-charge rounds is "HL." The shaped-charge round originally fired from the Pz.Kpfw. III Ausf. N's 75mm main gun received the designation Gr.38 HL, with improved versions being referred to as the Gr. 38 HL/A, HL/B, and HL/C.

A shaped-charge projectile's damage to a target comes from focusing the gases generated by the explosion at impact into a super-velocity, high-pressure molten jet that erodes armor by a combination of heat transfer (to melt the armor) and momentum transfer (which carries the molten armor/copper mixture from the charge liner away from the penetration site). Once the shaped-charge molten jet penetrates the armor of an enemy tank, hot gases, the blast concussion and fragmentation of the projectile, and the molten fragments of the tank's armor cause major damage to the interior of the vehicle.

German World War II shaped-charge projectiles lacked the penetrative abilities of the various KE projectiles then in use by the *Panzertruppen*, since the spinning imparted by the rifling in their gun tubes had a detrimental effect on the formation of the shaped-charge molten jet. The Germans tried various methods of countering the effects of spin on their shaped-charge warheads without much success. It was only after World War II that different armies managed to solve the problem of firing shaped-charge projectiles from rifled tank guns by fitting them with non-slipping bands in place of the normal rotating bands.

Production of the Pz.Kpfw. III Ausf. N began in June of 1942 and ended in August 1943, with almost 700 units completed. This was to be the last version. The Germans also used Ausf. J, L, and M chassis for conversion into the Ausf. N. The Pz.Kpfw. III Ausf. N continued in German military service as a fire-support vehicle for defending Tiger tank battalions and Panzergrenadier Divisions (specially trained infantry riding in armored halftracks or unarmored trucks) from enemy infantry units and towed antitank guns.

Sitting on a string of railroad flatcars are a number of German tanks whose crews seem to be enjoying the weather in their bathing trunks on a peaceful summer day. From front to back are a Pz.Kpfw. IV Ausf. D, a Pz.Kpfw. I Ausf. A., and a Pz.Kpfw. IV Ausf. C. *Patton Museum*

Recently restored and placed on display at the main entrance to the U.S. Army's Aberdeen Proving Ground, located in Aberdeen, Maryland, is a Pz.Kpfw. IV Ausf. D. It has the paint scheme and markings common to German tanks during the fighting in North Africa between 1940 and 1943. The tank is part of the large collection of military vehicles belonging to the U.S. Army Ordnance Museum that resides on the post. *Richard Isner*

The British army first noticed the 23-ton (20.7 metric ton) Pz.Kpfw. III Ausf. N in early 1943, as documented in this extract from a British army Technical Intelligence Summary dated January 15, 1943:

Another recent development is the appearance of Pz.Kw. IIIs mounted with what appears to be

the old short 7.5cm. Kw.K. These tanks have hull side loading doors and, apart from the gun barrel, appear to be identical with the Model L. Thus, even the recoil gear casing on the front of the mantlet and the armored barrel protecting sleeve are of the same pattern as provided on the Pz.Kw. III Model L for the 5cm. Kw.K. 39.

Pictured during a training exercise is a German army Pz.Kpfw. IV Ausf. D. The biggest improvement to this version of the tank was the increase in armor protection from 0.59 inch (15 millimeters) to 0.79 inch (20 millimeters) along the rear and sides of the vehicle. Frontal armor protection on the tank was 1.18 inches (30 millimeters). This soon proved to be insufficient, and the Germans began adding extra 1.18-inch (30-millimeter) armor plates to the front of the vehicle's hull and superstructure. *Patton Museum*

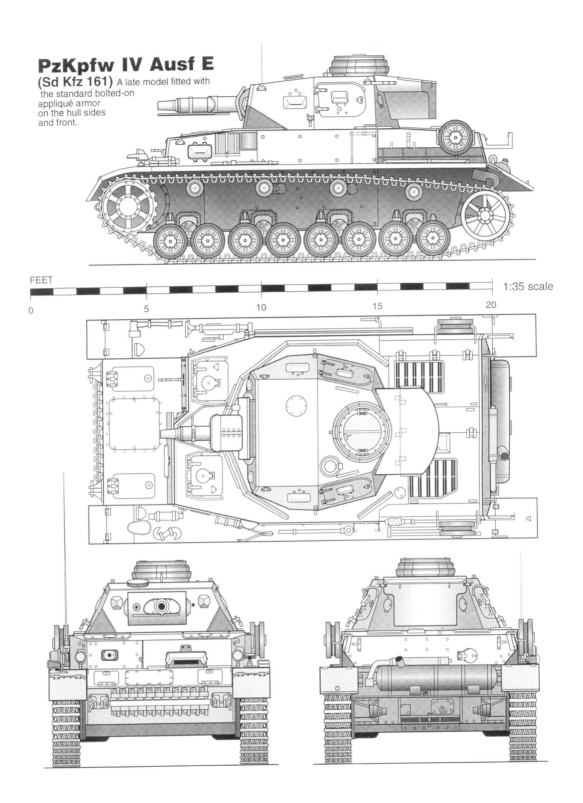

PzKpfw IV Ausf E

(Sd Kfz 161) A late model fitted with the standard bolted-on appliqué armor on the hull sides and front.

FEET

0   5   10   15   20

1:35 scale

The various external design features of the Pz.Kpfw. IV Ausf. E appear in this four-view line drawing. This version of the tank came with a new tank commander's cupola and an increased level of armor protection through a combination of up-armoring the vehicle itself and adding extra armor plates on that. Rotating the turret on the tank was done manually or by electric power. *George Bradford*

Because the low-velocity, short-tube 75mm main gun on the Pz.Kpfw. IV Ausf. A- through F-series tanks lacked sufficient penetrative powers, the German army had a long, high-velocity 75mm main gun mounted in an Ausf. F version of the tank. The tank was then designated the Pz.Kpfw. IV Ausf. G, an example of which is on display at the U.S. Army Ordnance Museum, with the early-style single-baffle muzzle brake. *Michael Green*

The April 1944 issue of the publication *Intelligence Bulletin* contains this statement, gleaned from a German prisoner of war regarding the tactical employment of the Pz.Kpfw. III Ausf. N:

> *Originally, it was planned that Pz.Kw. VIs [Tiger Is] should be supported by an equal number of Pz.Kw IIIs to provide local protection. The latter would move on the flanks of the main body of the Pz.Kw. VIs and cover them against hostile tank hunters attempting to attack them at close range. During an assault, the Pz.Kw. VIs would attack hostile heavy tanks battalions or heavy pill-boxes, and the Pz.Kw. IIIs would attack machine gun nests or lighter tanks. This method was altered in Sicily, where ground conditions repeatedly kept tanks to the roads and limited their usefulness—thereby decreasing the need for local protection. At least one battalion, which should have had nine of each type to a company, exchanged its Pz.Kw. IIIs for the Pz.Kw. VIs of another unit, after which the company was made up of 17 Pz.Kw. VIs only.*

Some early models of the Pz.Kpfw. IV series, originally armed with the short-tube, low-velocity 75mm main guns, were later up-gunned with the long-barrelled, high-velocity 75mm main gun. This Pz.Kpfw. IV Ausf. D, which forms part of the collection of the Tank Museum in Bovington, is an example of the upgrading process. The device fitted to the upper portion of the rear hull plate is an armored cover for the attached smoke grenade launchers. *Tank Museum–Bovington*

Pictured here is the driver's compartment of a Pz.Kpfw. IV Ausf. D. While the drivers of all Pz.Kpfw. IV-series tanks had an overhead hatch for entering and leaving their position, their seats were not adjustable in height. Therefore, the sole vision devices for the tank's driver were a small vision port, seen here in the vehicle front superstructure plate, as well as a vision port to his left side (in versions until the Ausf. H). Directly behind the driver's position are storage racks for some of the tank's main gun rounds. *Tank Museum–Bovington*

There were several command variants of the Panzer III, as well as artillery OP (observation post) models. It served these mission roles until the end of the war.

THE OTHER MEDIUM TANK: PZ.KPFW. IV

In January of 1934, the German army ordnance department approved the development of a larger and heavier five-man, gasoline-powered medium tank designated the Pz.Kpfw. IV. While the Pz.Kpfw. III's original mission role was as a tank killer, the Pz.Kpfw. IV was developed originally as a fire-support escort vehicle for the Pz.Kpfw. I, II, and III. This role appears in the tank's original designation as a *Begleitwagen*, shorted to B.W., which translates to escort tank. For this role, it was fitted with a low-velocity 75mm main gun officially designated the 7.5cm Kw.K. L/24. This short, 5.9-foot (1.80-meter) gun tube was intended mainly to fire HE rounds at enemy antitank guns and defensive positions.

Three firms bid for the contract to develop and build the Pz.Kpfw. IV for the German army. Rheinmetall Borsig, Krupp-Grusonwerk, and MAN submitted prototype vehicles for testing by the German army ordnance department. Krupp-Grusonwerk won the contract. The company built 35 pre-production Pz.Kpfw. IV Ausf. A prototypes between October and March of 1938. The prototypes were tested in battle during the invasions of Poland (September 1939), Norway (April 1940) and the Low Countries/France (May 1940). The Pz.Kpfw. IV Ausf. A was pulled from service by the German army before the invasion of the Soviet Union in June 1941.

Although it had originally specified an interleaved (overlapping) coil-spring road-wheel suspension system for the Pz.Kpfw. IV, the German army changed the requirement to a tandem road-wheel, torsion-bar suspension system. Krupp-Grusonwerk objected to this change and insisted on using eight sets of small tandem road wheels riding on leaf springs on either side of the hull. Rather than delay the fielding of the Pz.Kpfw. IV by arguing the point, the German army gave Krupp-Grusonwerk the okay to proceed with their in-house suspension system design. The irony of this decision was the fact that this was the same suspension system design rejected by the German army ordnance department for the Pz.Kpfw. III series.

The 18-ton (16.2 metric ton) Ausf A version of the Pz.Kpfw. IV (Sd.Kfz. 161) set the pattern for the first few versions of the vehicle, ranging from the Ausf. B through the Ausf. F. The maximum armor thickness was 0.8 inch (20 millimeters). The feature that remained part of the tank's design throughout all versions was a drum-shaped commander's cupola centered on the turret roof at the rear of the vehicle, similar to that mounted on most versions of the Pz.Kpfw. III. In this arrangement, the tank commander sat directly behind the main gun breech. The gunner was located to the right and the loader to the left of the breech.

The new Pz.Kpfw. IV Ausf. A tank was 18.4 feet (5.6 meters) long and 8.7 feet (2.65 meters) tall. The vehicle had a width of 9.5 feet (2.9 meters) and received power from a 250-horsepower, 12-cylinder, water-cooled Maybach 108TR gasoline engine. The tank's transmission provided five forward gears and one in reverse. Top speed of the

To counter the threat posed by the Red Army's 14.5mm antitank rifles penetrating the side hull armor of the Pz.Kpfw. III- and IV-series tanks, the German military began attaching thin, soft-steel plates to the exterior of their tank's hulls and turrets, as seen here on a Pz.Kpfw. IV Ausf. H. This simple, expedient measure effectively ended the problem posed by the Russian antitank rifles. *Patton Museum*

tank on a paved level road was 19 miles per hour (31 kilometers per hour). The operational range of the Pz.Kpfw. IV Ausf. A was listed as 93 miles (150 kilometers).

The short-barreled 75mm main gun fired several types of armor-piercing rounds, including an APC projectile with a muzzle velocity of only 1,260 feet per second (384 meters per second). In theory, this round and velocity could penetrate 1.4 inches (35 millimeters) of steel armor sloped at 30 degrees, at a range of 1,094 yards (1,000 meters). Panzer General Heinz Guderian wrote that the short-barreled 75mm gun on the Pz.Kpfw. IV was only

effective against the Red Army T34/76 medium tank if the German tank attacked it directly from the rear and managed to strike the grating just above the engine block—a somewhat impractical tactic in combat.

A World War II British army report, based on a captured German training manual, describes the crew duties of the Pz.Kpfw. IV:

The crew consists of five men: a commander, a gunner, a loader, a driver, and a wireless operator (radioman) who is also the hull machine-gunner.

Beside using soft-steel plates to stop the 14.5mm Red Army antitank rifles from penetrating the side hull armor of the Pz.Kpfw. III- and IV-series tanks, the Germans also came up with another arrangement that was equally effective. It consisted of wire mesh supported by simple metal tubing, which attached to either side of a tank's hull, as seen in this picture of a knocked-out Pz.Kpfw. IV Ausf. H. *Patton Museum*

On display at the Swiss Army Tank Museum is a Pz.Kpfw. IV Ausf. H with the standard double-baffle muzzle brake. An external spotting feature of this version of the Pz.Kpfw. IV series is the deletion of the small vision ports used by the driver and the radioman that were located on either side of the vehicle's superstructure. The Ausf. H version of the Pz.Kpfw. IV also came with a new, one-piece tank commander's overhead hatch. *Andreas Kirchoff*

The tank commander, who is an officer or senior noncom, is responsible for the vehicle and the crew. He indicates targets to the gunner, gives fire orders, and observes the fall of shots. He keeps a constant lookout for the enemy, observes the zone for which he is responsible, and watches for any orders from the commander's vehicle. In action, he gives his orders to the driver and wireless operator by intercommunication telephone and to the gunner and loader by touch signals or through a speaking tube. He receives orders by radio or flag, and reports to his commander by radio, signal pistol, or flag.

The gunner is the tank's commander's deputy. He fires the turret gun, the turret M.G. [machine gun], or the machine carbine, as ordered by the tank commander. He assists the tank commander in observation.

The loader loads and maintains the turret armament under the orders of the gunner. He is also responsible for care of ammunition, and when the cupola is closed, gives any flag signals required. He replaces the wireless operator if the latter becomes a casualty.

The driver drives the vehicle under the orders of the tank commander, or in accordance with orders received by radio from the commander's vehicle. So far as possible, he assists in observation, reporting over the intercommunication telephone the presence of the enemy or of any obstacles in the path of the tank. He watches the petrol [gas] consumption and is responsible to the tank commander for the care and maintenance of the vehicle.

The wireless operator operates the wireless set under the orders of the tank commander. In action,

The German Tank Museum demonstrates its restored Pz.Kpfw. IV Ausf. G. Captured by the British Army in 1943, it was returned to the German army in the 1960s as a gesture of goodwill between former opponents. *Thomas Anderson*

when not actually transmitting, he always keeps the radio set at "receive." He operates the inter-communication telephone and writes down any radio messages not sent or received by the tank commander. He fires the M.G. mounted in the front superstructure. He takes over the duties of the loader if the latter becomes a casualty.

MORE VERSIONS OF THE PZ.KPFW. IV APPEAR

The Ausf. B of the Pz.Kpfw. IV (Sd.Kfz. 161) series began rolling off the production lines in 1938 and incorporated a number of improvements to the first model, including a more powerful Maybach gasoline engine and thicker 1.2-inch (30-millimeter) frontal armor. The heavier armor raised the combat weight of the tank to about 19 tons (17.1 metric tons). The German army ordered 45 Pz.Kpfw. IV Ausf. Bs for delivery between April and September of 1938. However, Krupp-Grusonwerk was able to produce only 42 vehicles before they ran out of parts.

The Ausf. C Pz.Kpfw. IV (Sd.Kfz. 161) immediately followed the Ausf. B on the production lines. The minor changes included the substitution of the front machine

gun by a vision slot and pistol port. Production of the 134 Pz.Kpfw. IV Ausf. Cs ended in August of 1939.

The first three versions of the Pz.Kpfw. IV series (A, B, and C) had all been fitted with an internal mantlet, or gun shield, which had allowed bullet splash to enter the turret. To correct this design fault, the Pz.Kpfw. IV Ausf. D (Sd.Kfz. 161) featured a new, external mantlet. Other improvements to the Ausf. D included the reintroduction of the front superstructure-mounted 7.92mm machine gun and an increase in side and rear hull thickness from 0.6 inch (15 millimeters) to 0.8 inch (20 millimeters). Krupp-Gruson produced 229 Pz.Kpfw. IV Ausf. Ds between October 1939 and May 1941.

Combat experience similar to that of the Pz.Kpfw. III quickly demonstrated that the armor protection of the early model Pz.Kpfw. IVs was inadequate. As a quick fix, late production examples of the Pz.Kpfw. IV Ausf. D had extra armor plates either welded or bolted to the vehicle's hull, superstructure, and turret, at the factory. The crews of early-model Pz.Kpfw. IVs sometimes took it upon themselves to up-armor their vehicles with whatever they could find.

To redress this problem, the frontal armor of the Pz.Kpfw. IV Ausf. E (Sd.Kfz. 161) was 2 inches (50 millimeters) thick, with extra steel 1.2-inch (30 millimeter) armor plates bolted to the existing front superstructure armor and 0.8-inch-thick (20 millimeters) plates added to the sides of the hull and superstructure. This additional armor protection pushed the tank's weight up to almost 22 tons (19.8 metric tons). Krupp-Gruson completed 223 examples of the Pz.Kpfw. IV Ausf. E before the introduction of the Ausf. F (Sd.Kfz 161) of the Pz.Kpfw. IV series, which entered into production in April 1941.

The Pz.Kpfw. IV Ausf. F continued with progressive improvement to the armor protection levels of the tank. The lower front hull plate and the front of the superstructure and turret were all 2 inches (50 millimeters) thick. The sides of the superstructure were increased to 1.2 inches (30 millimeters), replacing the bolt-on armor plates.

NEW MAIN GUN

The Pz.Kpfw. IV Ausf. F originally appeared with the same low-velocity 75mm main gun with the short gun tube common to all its predecessors. The German army and Hitler had already given some thought to having an up-gunned Pz.Kpfw. IV take over the Pz.Kpfw. III's tank-killer role. The switch to the up-gunned Pz.Kpfw. IV took place long before the German invasion of the Soviet Union in June of 1941.

When the design requirements for the Pz.Kpfw. IV were first being set down, the German army had considered arming it with a high-velocity 75mm long-tube main gun to deal with a new generation of better-armed French tanks boasting 1.6-inch-thick (40 millimeters) steel armor. However, in the end, they

This former Syrian army Pz.Kpfw. IV Ausf. G was captured by the Israeli army in the 1973 Yom Kippur War, and was acquired in trade with the Israeli Army Tank Museum It now belongs to the Military Vehicle Technology Foundation in California. Syria acquired a number of rebuilt late-World War II Pz.Kpfw. IVs from Czechoslovakia, France, and Spain in the 1950s. *Michael Green*

PzKpfw IV Ausf J
(Sd Kfz 161/2) final production

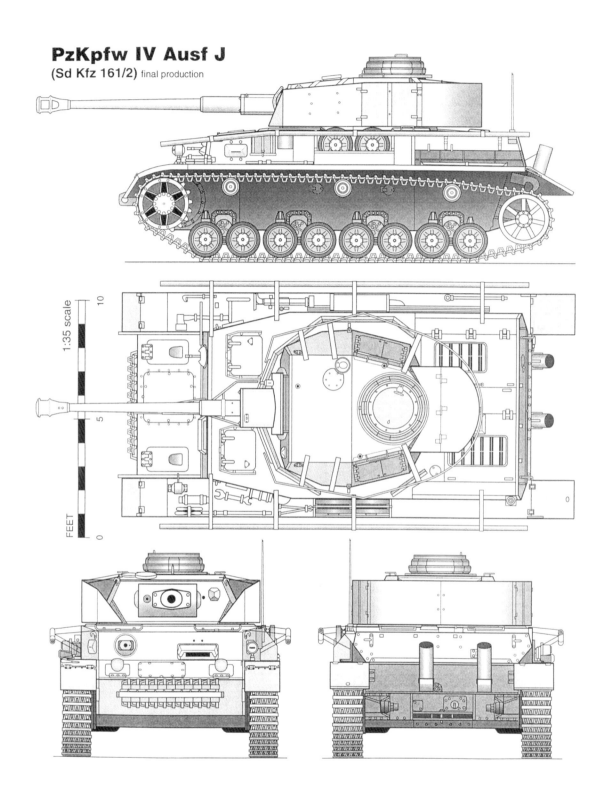

1:35 scale

FEET

A four-view line drawing illustrates the various external features of the Pz.Kpfw. IV Ausf. J, which include the lack of vision ports in the turret side doors. Another key spotting feature for the Ausf. J version of the Pz.Kpfw. IV series is the three upper track-return rollers, rather than the four seen on all previous models. *George Bradford* decided that AP rounds fired from the short-barreled 75mm gun would be sufficient, even though German military intelligence had discovered that the armor on French heavy tanks was actually thicker than 1.6 inches (40 millimeters).

As events transpired in France in the summer of 1940, it became clear that the smaller gun was unable to penetrate the armor of French Char B heavy tanks or British infantry-support Matilda tanks. In January of 1941, British tank units routed the Italian Army in North Africa with a small number of Matilda tanks because the Italian troops lacked an antitank weapon that could defeat the thick frontal armor of the British tanks. The following month, fearing that they would face the same fate, the German army ordered an up-gunned Pz.Kpfw. IV version with a long-tube 50mm main gun designated the 5cm Kw.K. 39 L/60.

While the 50mm main gun with the long gun tube would eventually go into service on the Pz.Kpfw. III series, an order for 50 units of the Pz.Kpfw. IV fitted with the same weapon was canceled. Obviously, somebody figured out that it would be a serious error to mount a 50mm main gun on a tank that had enough room to mount a much larger and more powerful weapon.

Krupp wasted no time in developing a high-velocity 75mm main gun with a long gun tube for the Pz.Kpfw. IV that could penetrate the thick 3.12-inch (78-millimeter) frontal armor on the British army Matilda tank. Unfortunately, the conservative German army ordnance department insisted that no tank main gun could extend over the front of a tank's hull for fear that it might suffer damage by striking an object. Krupp reluctantly shortened the gun tube on their new 75mm main gun to just 8.5 feet (2.59 meters), which reduced the gun's penetrative abilities. Krupp built only one example of the gun, officially designated the 7.5cm Kw.K. L/34.5, which was tested at the end of 1941.

Events in Russia soon overtook the Pz.Kpfw. IV Ausf. F up-gunning issue. It was now obvious that there was a pressing need for a long-tube 75mm gun on the Pz.Kpfw. IV to deal with the Red Army's T34/76 medium tank and KV series heavy tanks. The German army ordnance department's directive that no tank main gun could extend beyond the front hull of a tank quickly fell by the wayside, and Krupp, in cooperation with Rheinmetall, developed a new high-velocity 75mm tank main gun based on an existing towed 75mm antitank gun. The German designation for the modified gun as mounted on the

This destroyed and stripped Pz.Kpfw. IV Ausf. J shows the typical fate of most German tanks by the end of World War II. The tank will remain in place until the scrap dealers show up to cart it away. An interesting feature seen in this picture is the support brackets for the thin, soft-steel plates arranged around the outside of the tank's turret. *Patton Museum*

Pz.Kpfw. IV Ausf. F was the 7.5cm Kw.K. 40 L/43. It was 10.6 feet (3.23 meters) long.

Ammunition for the tank main gun was different from the towed version's ammunition. The cartridge case was shorter and fatter for the tank so that it could be loaded within the confines of the tank's turret.

The 2,426 feet-per-second (740 meters per second) muzzle velocity of armor-piercing-capped, ballistic-capped/high explosive (APCBC/HE) rounds fired from the new Ausf. F high-velocity 75mm main gun could penetrate 3.24 inches (81 millimeters) of steel armor sloped at 30 degrees at a range 1,094 yards (1,000 meters). The term ballistic cap, or the abbreviation "BC" in British military nomenclature, refers to a streamlined ballistic cap fitted over a piercing cap, which reduces drag (wind resistance). American military nomenclature in World War II did not differentiate between a standard APC round and one fitted with a ballistic cap.

The high explosives in the APCBC/HE shell fired from the 75mm main gun on the Pz.Kpfw. IV Ausf F offered

The other tank that proved superior to the Pz.Kpfw. III tank in both firepower and armor protection during the German invasion of France in May/June 1940, was the British army's Matilda Mk. II. It which featured a turret-mounted 40mm main gun and frontal armor up to 78mm thick. The Matilda Mk. II tank pictured here belongs to the collection of the Military Vehicle Technology Foundation located in Northern California. *Michael Green*

both advantages and disadvantages. The big advantage came after penetration, since the HE filler caused significantly more damage inside an enemy tank than achieved by an APCBC projectile without an HE filler. The disadvantage with an HE filler is that the internal cavity weakens the strength of the projectile's body and could result in less penetration being achieved compared to an APCBC projectile without an internal cavity for an HE filler.

From a British army report dated May 1942 comes this description of the effectiveness of German ABCBC/HE projectiles: "The German projectiles which have caused the greatest amount of damage to Allied tanks in the Western Desert campaigns have been the AP-HE type . . . . These projectiles at long range need only attain a partial penetration and the explosive charge can complete the destruction of at least the tank crew. At closer ranges the destructive effect is very great, where in many cases destruction of the tank is permanent."

The new main gun also fired a tungsten sub-caliber APCR round, achieving a muzzle velocity of 3,246 feet per second (990 meters per second) that could penetrate 3.48 inches (87 millimeters) of steel armor sloped at 30 degrees at a range of 1,094 yards (1,000 meters). The APCR round did not contain an HE filler. Other main-gun rounds employed by the Pz.Kpfw. IV Ausf F included a shaped-charge and HE round.

The Germans also developed a smoke round for the new 75mm main gun. The August 1944 issue of the publication *Intelligence Bulletin* described the use of smoke rounds by German tanks:

> As a rule, German tanks employ smoke shells to achieve surprise, to conceal a change of direction, and to cover their withdrawal. The shells normally are fired to land about 100 yards (91.4 meters) in front of an Allied force. There are no reports to indicate that smoke shells are used in range estimation. Smoke shells are fired from the 75mm guns of the Pz.Kpfw. IV and also, it is reported, from 88mm guns on other armored vehicles. Smoke shells are not fired by the Pz.Kpfw. II or Pz.Kpfw. III, both of which are equipped to discharge 'smoke pots' with a range of approximately 50 yards (45.7 meters). These pots are released electrically, and are employed chiefly to permit the tank to escape when caught by antitank fire.

To reduce recoil on the main gun, the new 75mm main gun on the Pz.Kpfw. IV Ausf. F came with a single-baffle spherical muzzle brake at the end of the gun tube. The purpose of a muzzle brake is to retard recoil. Muzzle brakes are no longer mounted on modern tanks because tanks have gotten so heavy (for armor protection purposes) that they can easily absorb greater recoil levels without the need for muzzle brakes.

GERMAN TANK COMMANDER INTERVIEW

In an interview with the authors of *Panzers At War*, Dr. Wolfgang Sterner, who commanded a variety of German medium tanks from the Pz.Kpfw. III to the Panther, described his time in service with the *Panzertruppen* during World War II:

What made you want to be a tanker in the German army?

The story is easy. I wanted to be a tank officer from the very beginning. Instead, I ended up, in spring 1942, as an officer aspirant [cadet] in an infantry unit. Then, to my surprise, nine months later I was transferred to a tank unit. They moved me right away to a field-training unit on the Russian front in the Orel area to Panzer Regiment 33. For the next three months, I received intensive training in tanks and their tactics.

Wolfgang Sterner as a young tank officer.

What I did not know at the time was all these preparations were made for the oncoming campaign of what you call the 'Battle of Kursk.' We were in the framework of the 9th Army and our division, the 9th Panzer Division, was in the center of the northern attack force, the XXXXVII Panzer Korps. I was commander of a Mark III medium tank with a 50mm long gun, later a Mark IV with the 75mm long gun. Our battalion had around 80 tanks at that time, Mark III and Mark IV.

Tell me about the Pz.Kpfw. IV tank. How did it compare to the Soviet T34 medium tank?

The question cannot be answered that easily. The improved Mark IV tank with a long-barrel 75mm gun and extra armor, including side skirts, was a reliable tank, and it was the workhorse of the German army. But, the T34 was still better in several ways. It was much faster. It had tremendous maneuverability under Russian conditions, and the gun on the tank was pretty good, too, but otherwise we were on even terms. We were better because each of our tanks had radio communication so that the tank could be better led. This was very important in a tank battle. With good communications and the proper leadership, you could easily take advantage of the right situation, which the Russians couldn't do. That was our main advantage over the Russian tanks. Their big advantage was that they usually had many more tanks.

While serving in the Pz.Kpfw. IV tank, did you ever think it would have been nicer if you had been equipped with the newer Panther tank?

At the time, in summer 1943, we knew about the Panther, but it was a completely new tank unproved in battle. It looked very impressive. Later on, a year later or so, of course, I was in favor of the Panther. It was an excellent tank in many ways. From the mechanical point, there still existed problems. Generally, the situation with our tanks was that they had superior guns, sights, and radio communications, etc., but the mechanical parts wore out more easily. Therefore, greater numbers were not ready for combat due, not to the result of any enemy actions, but to mechanical breakdowns.

Could you describe how it felt to be inside of tank in the middle of battle?

Before the battle begins, you tense up tremendously. Normally, this will end when the battle starts, since you will be too busy to be tense. Still, in the background, you will always have butterflies in your stomach, but it's getting less and less because you are 'too damn busy' as a tank commander to observe, to give orders and take orders, and the main thing is for survival. You do many things just because you have the right feeling; if you don't function well you are dead. Your eyes are popping out of your head in order to observe the battlefield to see whether any danger is reported or to watch out for your other tanks.

Of course, you have tension; whether you call it fear or not, I don't know. It's not that you are tension-free, but if you want to stay in control of yourself you must be able to reduce this tension to a degree that you are fully functional. This is especially true if you are in command of a tank. If you don't have that control, then you are not a tank leader at all.

As a tank leader, you generally yell at people; they look to you and if they see you are shaking up there or getting nervous, they lose confidence in you. So, you try to be as calm as possible all the time. It's not easy, I tell you that. Now, in a tank, of course, you communicate to most of them, to the driver and to the radio operator, only by your communication system. The gunner, of course, you can touch, and the loader, but the communication is important. And they talk to you, they help you to observe.

You stand there and watch the other tanks move and protect them by fire as they change their positions. When you break through the enemy positions, then all your tanks move and shoot like crazy. But, you usually don't hit anything, but psychologically the effect is tremendous. Tanks are running on and firing, and the shock effect on the enemy is very great.

Then, of course, the stress inside a tank is tremendous. It's humid, smelly, the fumes of the gun make you choke. You know that any minute, any second, you might get hit somewhere, and you always fear that you are trapped in that damn thing and you will burn to death and won't get out. That's the major fear among all tankers, that you'll be burned alive in your tank. Even if you get out of your burning tank, you may be killed by the enemy infantry. But, it's still better to fight for your life outside your tank than burn to death within it.

Did you lose any tanks in battle?

Yes, in all my tank life, I lost three tanks by burning out. In the first battle, I had hits. I was hit several times but not to the degree that the tank burned or blew up. Sometimes, you see the rounds coming. But, you cannot tell exactly where it hits you. You are aware the tank is being hit some place because it shakes considerably, and then you ask around and the crew reports back. But, if you are hit to a degree that the tank burns, that's different. Then you hear and see an explosion at the time the high-velocity projectile will penetrate into the crew compartment; it depends on the type of ammunition. The damage inside the tank is caused by the impact, the fragments of plate knocked off during penetration, and their own effects when they bounce around inside the tank. In such cases, the tank looks inside like a slaughterhouse, blood all over.

The first time I was in a Mark IV, we had to counterattack a major Russian attack of T34s and heavier tanks. We were fighting tank against tank, and they got me. We were in firing position and we had stopped, since we couldn't fire accurately on the move in those days. Then we got the order from our platoon leader: 'You start firing from the left and we start from the right side, and then you are on your own.' Then you give orders to your gunner and he turns the turret in the direction of the enemy. The battle starts and you fire and fire until you think you hit an enemy tank. They don't always blow up right away. But, if you see him stop firing, you assume a hit. Although sometimes they start firing again, then you fire again. During such a battle, I was hit by a T34. He caught me from the side. My tank began to burn. The members of the crew escaped, though wounded.

Being hit in a tank while in battle, I would compare it to a big car crash. It's a tremendous shock and noise inside the tank. The tank becomes dark or you see flames, [and] the engine stops. Then you hear the crying of the wounded people if they are still able to cry. The smell of course, and the flumes, first impels you to open your hatch, because the tank will blow up in seconds. As a tank commander, however, you shouldn't do that without checking on your crew. You must always try to save the wounded inside your tank if possible at all. If you don't do that, you will lose the leadership of your crew very soon. Sometimes you have no choice, if the tank starts to burn all over right away you must get out quickly. Losing your crew or part of it in such manner is really hard to take.

Did German tankers ever play dead on the battlefield to lure unsuspecting enemy tanks within firing range?

Possible, but this is not a technique that was officially taught to us. This was not, you know, in a chapter of German tank training manuals. A tank alone is like a sitting duck. If you were temporary disabled in the tank, or you had problems with your gun and you had a chance to fight again, you would do it. It is completely dependent on the individual tank commander and the general situation, of course.

Was it normal practice in combat to shoot at the crew of an enemy tank when they were forced to leave their vehicle?

Every nation does that. Out-coming tank crews are target number one, if they try to escape. So did we. Of course, nobody thought much about that. In the next moment, there might be another enemy tank, and then they are shooting at you and they are trying to kill you. So, in battle, there is no mercy on either side. The basic law of combat: 'kill or be killed.'

After seeing how the Russians fought, did you see any differences in the way the Americans, the British, or the Canadians used their tanks?

The tactics the Western Allies used were completely different from the Russians. They made only very careful moves. Their tanks were rarely used for mass breakthroughs like the Russians often did. They were only used in step-by-step operations, to drill themselves through the German lines and to wear us out. From their point of view, it probably was the right tactic saving blood. From a German tanker's point of view, they moved very carefully, maybe sometimes too carefully. The moment they recognized us and we started to fire, usually they stopped and moved backwards into hiding, and then the fighter-bombers would come. In most cases, they wouldn't face us. They didn't have to face us; they did it the other way.

Could you describe American World War II tank tactics from your viewpoint as a German tank commander?

I can tell you about American tactics because I experienced them over and over again. When they attacked us, their tanks usually came first. Sometimes they had infantry on top of them if they felt relatively safe. Usually, they came rather slowly. They would move from one position to another, some tanks moving while others gave them fire protection. After my first rounds, they usually tried to take cover and then to figure out our position. If they considered the enemy fire too heavy, they pulled back. They would then call in these small, slow-moving artillery observation planes. We hated those like hell because there was no possibility for us to shoot them down. If you fired at them, you would give away your position; besides, with

Krupp-Gruson, Vomag, and Nibelungenwerke produced 437 Pz.Kpfw. IV Ausf. F units between early 1941 and early 1942—all armed with the short-tube 75mm main gun. As the factories starting up-gunning the Pz.Kpfw. IV Ausf. F tanks, there was an evolving change in the tank's designation. At one point, the German army decided to designate the tank the Pz.Kpfw. IV Ausf. F2 (Sd.Kfz. 161/1) in order to distinguish it from the original small-gun version, which became the Ausf. F1 for a time. The German army eventually referred to all long-barreled Ausf. F versions of the tank as the Pz.Kpfw. IV Ausf. G (Sd.Kfz 161/2). Production of the 1,900 Pz.Kpfw. IV Ausf. G vehicles took place between early 1942 and the summer of 1943.

In the summer of 1942, the factories building the Pz.Kpfw. IV Ausf. G began welding additional 1.2-inch

our machine guns, we couldn't reach them anyway. We didn't have enough anti-aircraft, 2cm [20mm] with which to hit those planes. When you saw them, you knew you were in trouble—you knew what was coming. Then pretty soon, it was coming—either heavy artillery fire, or planes, or both.

What did you fear more, the artillery or the fighter-bombers?

The fighter-bomber, definitely, because they were constantly over us if the weather allowed it, making it practically impossible to move during daytime. They made any movement damn near impossible. With artillery fire, you took your chances. Heavy artillery fire shakes you up. But, it does not harm your tank so much. It is a strain on the nerves because it makes an entire tank shake, but you could maneuver and move to a different position.

But if a fighter-bomber spotted you, you were usually finished. Not all the time; sometimes they ran out of ammunition, or sometimes they had to turn back because their fuel was gone or the weather became worse. If they had lots of fuel and lots of ammunition and the skies stayed clear, they kept coming after you, over and over again, until the bitter end.

On one occasion, I lost three of my tanks to six American fighter-bombers. We had performed an attack through a small German village. Only a few Panther and Mark IVs were left to do the job. When we started, we were rather successful pushing through and wiping out any American resistance. It was cloudy, then it cleared up, and in that moment, the fighter-bombers were above us. It was a road with a wooded hill on the left side. On the right side was wet swampy ground—no way to escape. They started to circle and then came down—six planes, one after the other with rockets and bombs. First, they hit and destroyed two tanks of my task force. A little bit later, my tank was hit, too. It burned and exploded.

Did they hit you with bombs or rockets?

Rockets, I saw them coming. They had the rockets under the wings. I believe three or four under each one. If it hits you directly behind the turret or on the turret, then of course you had no chance. The explosion was so strong that it threw me, standing in the turret, out of the turret. I was unconscious for a short time. Two members of my crew died in the tank. One became seriously wounded, and one escaped almost unharmed.

(30 millimeters) steel armor plates onto the existing 2-inch-thick (50 millimeters) front hull and superstructure of the vehicles. In April of 1943, the factories began bolting on the extra 1.2-inch-thick (30 millimeters) steel armor plates to the front hull and superstructure of the Pz.Kpfw. IV Ausf. G rather than welding them. That same month, the factories began installing a new, even longer high-velocity 75mm main gun on the tank.

The German designation for the new 75mm main with the even longer gun tube was 7.5cm Kw.K. 40 L/48. It came with a new double-baffle muzzle brake. The longer 11.8-foot (3.6-meter) gun tube increased the weapon's muzzle velocity and boosted the projectile's ability to penetrate the armor of enemy tanks. An APCBC projectile fired from the weapon could punch a hole through 3.4 inches (85 millimeters) of steel armor sloped at 30 degrees, at a

Half-hidden in the weeds of the Bulgarian Army Museum's open-air collection of military vehicles is this Pz.Kpfw. IV Ausf. J. This proved to be the last production version of the series, and it came off the production lines between the summer of 1944 and the end of the war in Europe. Besides Bulgaria, a few other countries that were friendly to Nazi Germany received the Pz.Kpfw. IV Ausf. J, including Spain and Romania. *Thomas Anderson*

range of 1,094 yards (1,000 meters). An APCR projectile fired from this could penetrate 3.9 inches (97 millimeters) of steel armor sloped at 30 degrees at a range of 1,094 yards (1,000 meters).

The gunner on the Pz.Kpfw. IV Ausf. F and the follow-on versions acquired their targets with a TZF 5f articulated telescope mounted to the left of the tank's main gun. German optical gun sights were far superior to anything the Western Allies or the Red Army mounted on their tanks during World War II.

Tom Sator, an M4 Sherman medium tank crewman who served in the U.S. Army's 4th Armored Division in Western Europe from late 1944 through the end of the war, remembers his first chance to look through the gunner's sight on a Pz.Kpfw. IV with the long 75mm main gun tube:

There was always a lot of talk about the effectiveness of the German tank guns against us. It is true that they had to stop to fire, but they started firing from 1,200 to 1,500 yards (1,096 to 1,371 meters). Their first shot was always a hit. We, on the other hand, had to get within 500 to 600 yards (457 to 548 meters) to be within effective firing distance, and even our best gunners needed at least two shots before they could score a hit.

Our CO (commanding officer), Captain Jimmy Leach, sent the platoon sergeant down to my tank during one of the lulls between German artillery barrages, and he hollered up, 'Hey Sator, you speak German?' 'Yeah, why?' I answered. 'The radio in that abandoned German tank (Pz.Kpfw. IV) back there is alive. Captain wants you to listen and see

what they are talking about.' So, I went with him. Sure enough, when we got there, you could hear the radio squawking. I climbed in and put the gunner's earphones on. It was difficult to hear, and because the guy was talking in a strange dialect, I could understand only a few words here and there. Then I saw the gun-sight and I figured I might as well look through it while I was there, and as soon as I did, almost immediately, the realization came to me why the German tank gunners were so accurate. 'Shit, I wanna go home' is the only thing that I could think of at the moment. Their sights were so far superior to ours that we didn't stand a chance.

When a tank gunner takes aim through his optical sight at a target, he is typically looking for the center of vulnerability of that target. On many targets it will be the exact center, but this is not always the case. The center of vulnerability will vary with the type of target and the angle engaged. For example, the thickest armor on tanks is on the front superstructure (upper hull) and turret, while the sides and rear tend to be much thinner, making them much more vulnerable. Whenever possible, tank gunners of all armies learn to aim at these parts of an enemy tank. German tankers were instructed to face their attacker head-on whenever possible and to never offer them a broadside target. If only the front of an enemy tank is in view, all tank gunners learn that the center of vulnerability is the enemy tank's turret ring, were the turret and superstructure (upper hull) join.

During the production run of the Pz.Kpfw. IV Ausf. G, a host of other minor changes and improvements

This French army Char B1 bis heavy tank rushing into action during the German invasion of France. It featured a hull-mounted 75mm gun with limited traverse and a turret-mounted 47mm gun; either weapon could penetrate the armor on any German tanks then in service. The Char B1 bis also featured frontal armor thick enough to be completely impervious to the projectiles fired from the 37mm main guns then in service on the Pz.Kpfw. III-series tanks. *Tank Museum–Bovington*

appeared. One of the most noticeable changes made to the Ausf. G version of the Pz.Kpfw. IV occurred in 1943, when thin soft-steel plates were introduced. These plates attached to the sides of the tank's hull and surrounded three sides of the tank's turret. They were designed to stop penetration by 14.5mm AP bullets fired from Red Army antitank rifles, which first began appearing in large numbers on the battlefield in late 1942. The adoption of the thin-armored skirting on the Pz.Kpfw. IV Ausf. G was mirrored on many of the remaining Pz.Kpfw. III vehicles still in German army service in 1943.

A wire-mesh screen on either side of the hull of the Pz.Kpfw. IV Ausf. G and later models was tested but not mounted until later. Both the soft metal plates and the wire-mesh screen were collectively called *Schürzen* (skirting) and served the same purpose. While originally designed to defeat 14.5mm projectiles, they might have also provided some limited standoff protection from Allied infantry antitank weapons firing shaped-charged warheads, such as the American Bazooka or the British army's projector infantry antitank (PIAT).

German tankers had to accept operational problems that resulted from the constant up-armoring and up-gunning of medium tanks. A German prisoner of war (POW or P/W), in a 1944 British army report, described some of the issues that arose due to the numerous modifications:

> [The] P/W refers to loss of maneuverability and speed of Pz.Kwk. III and IV owing to the increased weight, mainly due to thicker armor and bigger guns. He says that the [torsion-bar-equipped] Pz.KwK. III has stood up well, but that the [leaf-sprung] Pz.Kw. IV has become nose-heavy as a result of the fitting of the 7.5cm long gun, to such an extent that the front springs [are] always bent and the tank [sways] about.

THE END OF THE LINE

The Ausf. H version of the Pz.Kpfw. IV (Sd.Kfz. 161/2) followed the Pz.Kpfw. IV Ausf. G into production. The 3,774 Ausf. H units produced between early 1943 and mid-1944 by Krupp-Grusonwerk, Vomag, and Nibelungenwerke made it the most numerous version of the Pz.Kpfw. IV series. The Ausf. H retained the same 75mm main gun as the late-production versions of the Ausf. G. The hull and superstructure frontal armor thickness was increased to 3.2 inches (80 millimeters). The turret frontal armor thickness remained at 2 inches (50 millimeters).

The final version of the Pz.Kpfw. IV series was the Ausf. J (Sd.Kfz. 161/2), which first entered production in June of 1944—the same month that the Allied armies invaded occupied France. Unlike the Pz.Kpfw. IV Ausf. F through H built by a consortium of Krupp-Gruson, Vomag, and Nibelungenwerke, the Ausf. J was built solely by Nibelungenwerke. Krupp-Gruson and Vomag were then busy building turretless tank destroyers for the German army.

The Pz.Kpfw. IV Ausf. J looked very much like the Ausf. G and was armed with the same 75mm main gun. Most of the changes were internal, such as the elimination of the electric turret-traverse device and the auxiliary engine that powered it. The extra volume was taken up by a manual traverse and another fuel tank to increase the vehicle's operating range. Improvements included thicker armor on the turret roof and the addition of a small mortar that could fire smoke or anti-personnel grenades. Nibelungenwerke built the last 50 or so units of the Pz.Kpfw. IV Ausf. J in April of 1945, the same month the war in Europe ended. By war's end, the total number of Pz.Kpfw. IV-series tanks numbered over 9,000, making it the most numerous of the German tanks to see service during World War II.

An early-production Panther Ausf. D tank appears ready for a test ride. Notice the tarp covering the tank's gun tube and mantlet to prevent the enemy from discovering any design details on the new tank should the photograph fall into enemy hands. Like all German tanks, the Panther D would go through a continuing series of design improvements throughout its production run. *Patton Museum*

One of the hallmarks of the new, simplified hull design of the Panther Ausf. G was the elimination of the welded-on armor wedges located at the rear of the superstructure's side hull plates. In their place, new, thicker superstructure hull side plates appeared that featured a slight taper from rear to front, to cover the area once protected by the welded-on armor wedge. This new design feature is clearly evident on this Panther Ausf. G on display in a Belgian town. *Andreas Kirchhoff*

CHAPTER THREE

PANTHER TANKS

BEFORE THE GERMAN ARMY INVADED THE Soviet Union in June of 1941, the Pz. Kpfw. III and IV medium tanks of the *Panzertruppen* had dominated the battlefield, due in large part to their superior tactics and training. However, this confidence would begin to ebb during a series of battles near the small Russian town of Mzensk in October 1941, when the German army's 4th Panzer Division had the misfortune of encountering a well-led brigade of Red Army T34/76 medium tanks, supported by a few KV-1 heavy tanks.

In the ensuing engagements, the sloped 1.8-inch (45 millimeters) frontal armor of the roughly 26-ton (23.58 metric tons) Russian T34/76 medium tank and the even thicker frontal armor on the roughly 43-ton (39 metric tons) Russian KV-1 heavy tanks successfully resisted penetration by the German tank main guns. This left the *Panzertruppen* defenseless against the 76.2mm main guns mounted on the Russian tanks, whose armor-piercing rounds easily penetrated the relatively thin armor of the Pz.Kpfw. III and IV medium tanks. When the Russian tanks finally departed the Mzensk area a week later, they left behind an array of destroyed German equipment,

including 133 tanks, 49 artillery pieces, and 15 half-track prime movers (towing vehicles) with ammunition.

The news of this one-sided, though minor, engagement at Mzensk quickly reached General Heinz Guderian, Panzer Group 2 commander, who oversaw the operations of the 4th Panzer Division. Guderian immediately alerted the German armaments ministry of the danger posed by the Russian T34/76. Based on Guderian's report, the armaments ministry convened to address the imminent threat to the success of the German war effort caused by its failure to maintain technical superiority on the battlefield.

Mzensk was not the first battle between Red Army T34/76 tanks and the *Panzertruppen*. Elements of the German 18th Panzer Division engaged and destroyed a small number of T34/76 tanks on July 3, 1941. The commander of the panzer division involved in the fracas quickly grasped the significance of this new Russian tank design and provided General Heinz Guderian with two captured examples to inspect. Guderian no doubt came to the same conclusion as the panzer divisional commander had, but Guderian also had to worry about a great many other

PzKpfw V, Ausf D (SdKfz 171)
"Panther" Early Production

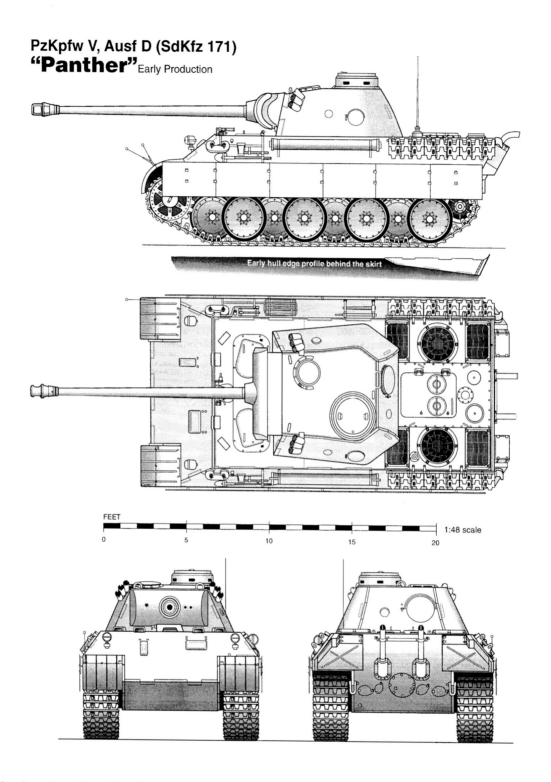

Early hull edge profile behind the skirt

FEET

0   5   10   15   20   1:48 scale

These drawings show the various design features of the early-production Panther D tanks. The smoke-grenade launchers on the turret disappeared from production units of the vehicle starting in June 1943, because combat experience showed that small-arms fire could detonate them and force the crew to abandon their vehicle. Also visible is the small, circular door in the turret wall used by the vehicle commander to talk to those outside the vehicle. *George Bradford*

Pictured on a Henschel production line are several Panther Ausf. D tank hulls. Like all German-manufactured tanks in World War II, their power came from a water-cooled Maybach gasoline engine, located in the rear of the tank's hull. Of the three compartments seen in the rear hulls of the Panther Ausf. Ds in this picture, the engine was located in the center compartment and the radiators and fans in the two side compartments. *Patton Museum*

become painfully obvious to the *Panzertruppen* and their leaders.

FIRST IMPRESSIONS OF THE T34/76

In November of 1941, weapons experts from the German armaments ministry inspected captured examples of the T34/76, now much feared by the Germans. Ministry experts were impressed by the extensive use of sloped armor, the large-caliber main gun, large road wheels, and wide tracks.

The sloped armor on the T34/76 provided two advantages in protecting a tank. First, highly sloped armor deflects incoming projectiles so that they do not penetrate the vehicle. In addition, the geometry of a sloped plate is such that its thickness when measured from a horizontal plane is greater than the perpendicular thickness of the plate itself. That extra thickness of a sloped plate with reference to a horizontal plane—a measurement known as the "armor basis"—provides a higher effective armor thickness to incoming projectiles on horizontal trajectories. The design of the Pz.Kpfw. I through Pz.Kpfw. IV presented mostly flat armor plates aligned perpendicularly to the line of fire of enemy gunners. This design made the German tanks far more vulnerable in combat than Red Army T34/76 tanks employing sloped armor.

The larger road wheels used by the T34/76 minimized rolling resistance and resisted mud and snow buildup. Clearly, the designers of the Russian tank had a much more realistic picture of the terrain than did the Germans.

Large road wheels, sloped armor, and other advanced features displayed on the T34s were innovations pioneered by an American inventor named J. Walter Christie in the 1920s. The American military was not interested in buying Christie's designs in large numbers, so he sought out foreign buyers. The Russians liked what they saw and copied Christie's many tank design features for their own use. The *Panzertruppen* were aware of the T34/76 heritage and even referred to the Russian medium tank as the "Christie tank" in some wartime reports.

The purpose of tracks on a combat vehicle is to spread a vehicle's weight over a large ground area so heavy vehicles can traverse soft and rough terrains. By using the widest practical tracks, tank designers reduce the ground pressure. Ground pressure is the gross vehicle weight divided by the track area on the ground. Wider tracks lower the ground pressure, which allows a tracked

larger and more important issues at the time, such as keeping his panzer group moving forward.

During the early stages of the German invasion of the Soviet Union, the Russians had not fared well against the Germans. What T34/76 tanks they had in service went into action against the invading German armies in very small groups. Only when a larger number of T34/76 tanks became available and finally massed together to engage the Germans at Mzensk using German-type tank tactics did the true fighting potential of the vehicle

PzKpfw V, Ausf A (SdKfz 171)
"Panther" Mid Production

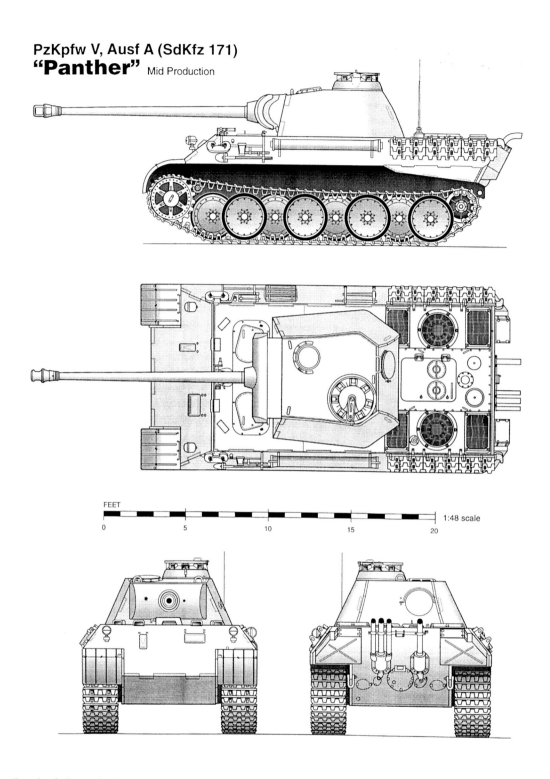

FEET

1:48 scale

0   5   10   15   20

The Panther Ausf. A was basically an unmodified Panther Ausf. D chassis fitted with an improved turret. The improved turret lacked the pistol ports seen in the sides and rear wall of the Ausf. D turret and the small circular communication opening on the vehicle commander's side of the Ausf. D turret. The most noticeable change to the new Ausf. A turret was the addition of a newly designed 4-inch-thick (100 millimeters) cast-steel armored vehicle commander's cupola. *George Bradford*

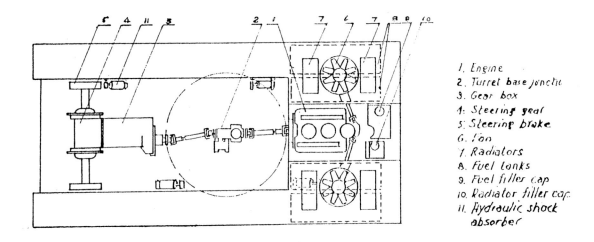

1. Engine
2. Turret base junctio..
3. Gear box
4. Steering gear
5. Steering brake
6. Fan
7. Radiators
8. Fuel tanks
9. Fuel filler cap
10. Radiator filler cap
11. Hydraulic shock absorber

This hand-drawn overhead view of a Panther tank hull from a British army World War II report shows the layout of the various automotive components, as well as the location of two shock absorbers. The drivetrain traveled from the engine compartment (underneath the turret basket) and connected to the transmission of the vehicle mounted in the forward hull. *Tank Museum–Bovington*

vehicle to carry more payload (or armor) than wheeled vehicles.

The wide tracks of the T34/76 enabled it to carry relatively heavy armor over soft terrains. In contrast, the prewar-designed Pz.Kpfw. I through IV had very narrow tracks (and a correspondingly higher ground pressure). Red Army T34/76 tanks passed easily over the same terrains that bogged down German light and medium tanks. The T34/76 proved so mobile in snow that the *Panzertruppen* nicknamed it the "Snow King."

The large-caliber main gun reflected the Soviet designers' strong belief that the primary purpose of the tank was the destruction of enemy tanks on the battlefield. One method to increase the lethality of any gun is to lengthen the barrel. This results in higher projectile velocity and improves the penetrating power of the tank round. The long main-gun barrel overhung the front of the vehicle. Prior to the encounters with the T34/76, German tank designers had avoided overhanging gun barrels because the front-heavy design created shipping and transit problems and increased the chance of barrel being damaged on rough or confining terrain.

The Christie suspension and long tracks on the T34/76 stabilized the vehicle enough to make a front-heavy weapon practical. It should be noted that Christie's design made it much easier to tailor suspension damping, making for less oscillation and better stability than other types of suspension systems. Additionally, the Christie design provided long rebound strokes, which improved the riding characteristics of a tank.

THE GERMAN RESPONSE

Based on their evaluation of the T34/76, the German armaments ministry staff quickly settled on a design and manufacturing plan to field a new medium tank for the *Panzertruppen*. Their basic specifications required a 75mm main gun, a gross vehicle weight of 30 to 35 tons (27 to 31.5 metric tons), a top speed of 35 miles per hour (56.3 kilometers per hour), and armor thicknesses of 2.4 inches (60 millimeters) on the front and 1.6 inches (40 millimeters) on the sides. In late November of 1941, the German firms of Daimler-Benz and MAN were commissioned to design the chassis for the new medium tank.

German production tanks had traditionally featured rear-mounted gasoline-powered engines and front transmissions. In a departure from this tradition, Daimler-Benz's final prototype featured a rear-mounted diesel engine close-coupled to the transmission, similar to the powertrain configuration of the T34/76. This in turn required that the turret be placed farther forward than other German tanks of the period. The Christie-style

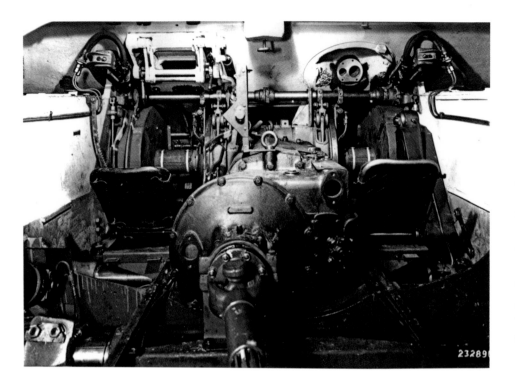

This picture taken inside a turretless Panther Ausf. A shows the front of the vehicle's hull, with the transmission mounted in place and the drivetrain extending rearward. The driver's position is on the left of the transmission, and the instrument panel is on top of the transmission. On the right side of the transmission is the radioman's position. The tank's radio, normally positioned on top of the transmission, does not appear in this picture.
Tank Museum–Bovington

suspension system consisted of large dual road wheels supported by external lower-hull springs. In this and many other ways, the Daimler-Benz prototype was a German copy of the T34/76.

The final MAN prototype chassis reflected more conventional German design features, with a rear-mounted gasoline-powered engine and a front transmission. The placement of the turret at the center of the vehicle min-imized the gun-barrel overhang, again following tradi-tional tank design practice up to that time. The only major break with tradition was the employment of sloped armor plates; earlier German tank chassis tended to be box-like, with a great many flat armor plates for protec-tion. Like the T34/76 medium tank, the prototype MAN chassis also featured much wider tracks than seen on prior German medium tanks.

MAN designers stuck to tradition for the suspension design, proposing large, overlapping road wheels sup-ported by transversely mounted high-strength spring-steel torsion bars spanning the bottom of the hull. Torsion bar suspensions and overlapping road wheels had first appeared on pre-World War II German half-track designs in the late 1930s.

In theory, the overlapping road-wheel configuration offered a more even distribution of loads along a track's length, thus contributing to a lower ground pressure.

In practice, the advantages were small relative to the disadvantages. In winter, mud packed tightly between the wheels, which then froze at night, rendering the ve-hicles immobile until the crews could dislodge the frozen muck with picks, crowbars, welding tools, and even small antipersonnel hand grenades. Another disadvantage was lower track life owing to the continual side-to-side "working" of the track.

The contract for the design of the turret for the *Panzertruppen*'s new medium tank went to the German firm of Rheinmetall. Their design featured a 5-inch-thick (125 millimeters) cast steel cylindrical gun mantle that ex-tended almost across the width of the turret front. The side and rear armor plates of the hexagonal-shaped turret was 1.8 inches (45 millimeters) thick, sloped at 25 degrees. The armored side plates bent inward near the back of the turret to meet the edges of a comparatively narrow rear armored plate.

Hitler took a personal interest in the evaluation of the Daimler-Benz and MAN prototypes for the new medium tank chassis. He was impressed with the Daimler-Benz prototype, placing an initial order for 200 production units in March 1942. This greatly frustrated the tank de-sign office of the German army's ordnance department, which had not yet completed its careful evaluation based on the needs of the *Panzertruppen*. The German army's

On display at a German museum is a late-production Panther Ausf. A. The glacis plate on all the various models of the Panther tank was 3.2 inches (80 millimeters) thick and sloped at 55 degrees. The 75mm main gun mounted on the tank was just a bit more than 19 feet long (5.8 meters) and fired electrically from a control handle on the gunner's elevating handwheel. *Mert Wreford*

ordnance department eventually picked the MAN chassis design in early May of 1942. The Daimler-Benz order for 200 vehicles quietly disappeared with Hitler's approval.

A major reason for the choice of the MAN chassis was that the Rheinmetall turret did not fit on the Daimler-Benz chassis. Daimler-Benz insisted that it could quickly design and build a suitable turret for their chassis, but the risk of running behind schedule was deemed to high. The first production vehicles were required to be ready for fielding by December of 1942.

The *Panzertruppen* did not like the Daimler-Benz prototype vehicle for a number of reasons, one being the length of the main gun tube, which projected a great distance over the front of the hull. There was genuine concern among many in the German military that this could result in frequent friendly-fire incidents, since German tankers and antitank gun crews might, in the heat of battle, mistake the vehicle for a Russian tank, since, up to that time, German tank main guns did not protrude over their front hulls.

INTO SERVICE

The German army ordered the first pre-production MAN chassis on May 15, 1942. The official designation of the new vehicle was Pz.Kpfw. V Panther Ausf. D (Sd.Kfz. 171). The name "Panther" came from the Panther Commission,

the small group of tank designers and engineers that helped set the requirements for the vehicle.

Adding to the designation confusion, the prefix "Pz.Kpfw. V" was phased out of use in February of 1944, on Hitler's order. In most German wartime reports, the vehicle went just by the name "Panther." American and British military reports generally referred to it as the Mark V.

By August 1942, MAN had presented the German army with two pre-production Panther tanks for testing. One came without a turret, while the other had the specified Rheinmetall turret fitted. In its haste to field the Panther Ausf. D, the German army ignored a number of serious automotive design faults identified during testing with these two pre-production prototypes and ordered the vehicle into full series production in November of 1942.

In order to meet the German army's goal of having 250 Panther Ausf. Ds in service by May of 1943, other German firms tooled up to build the vehicle. These included Daimler-Benz, Maschinenfabrik Niedersachsen [of] Hanover (MNH), and Henschel. The rush to production was necessary to support Hitler's and the German military high command's plan to launch a massive summer offensive against the Red Army, codenamed *Operation Zitadelle* (Operation Citadel). The armored spearhead of that operation was to be the new Panther Ausf. D and the Tiger I heavy tank.

Taking part in a public demonstration is the late-production Panther Ausf. A tank belonging to the Deutsches Panzermuseum (German Tank Museum). This particular example is a *Panzerbefehlswagen*, a command-tank version of the Panther tank series. It features two extra radios and two additional antennas, one mounted on the turret roof and the other on the rear of the hull. *Thomas Anderson*

The production Panther Ausf. Ds differed from the original MAN pre-production vehicles in several details. The most important change was an increase in the upper front superstructure plate from 2.4 inches (60 millimeters) thick to 3.2 inches (80 millimeters). The slope remained at 55 degrees from horizontal. The armor thickness increase resulted in a weight increase to 43 tons (39 metric tons) and dangerously overstressed the suspension system, engine, transmission, and drivetrain. Tentative plans to add even more armor to the Panther series passed from consideration because the vehicle had reached its design limits.

The only exception to this rule forbidding adding any extra armor to the Panther Ausf. D chassis occurred in April of 1943, when some thin, soft-steel removable plates were attached to either side of the vehicle's super-structure by brackets. The intended purpose of these plates was to stop 14.5mm AP rounds fired by Russian antitank rifles.

Through intense effort, the German army managed to have 200 Panther Ausf. Ds ready for service by July 5, 1943, for the start of *Operation Zitadelle*. This was Hitler's failed attempt to turn the tide of battle against the Red Army in the summer of 1943. What Hitler and the German army did not know was that Russian factories had already ramped up to build 1,000 T34/76 medium tanks per month. Only 850 Panther Ausf. Ds entered German military service between January of 1943 and September of that same year.

COMBAT IMPRESSIONS

The combat debut of the Panther Ausf. D during *Operation Zitadelle* proved to be a major disappointment for the

German army. During the first few days of fighting, the number of operational Panther Ausf. Ds dropped to fewer than a dozen vehicles. Those not lost to mechanical breakdowns saw destruction at the hands of the enemy. One German army officer observed that many of the untrained *Panzertruppen* failed to keep their vehicle's thick, sloping frontal armor turned toward enemy fire. This basic tactical blunder exposed the thinner side armor of the Panther Ausf. Ds to enemy fire and significantly increased combat losses.

A German wartime document reminding the *Panzertruppen* of the vulnerability of the Panther to side attack read, "It is particularly important to ensure flank protection for the sensitive sides of the Panther tank. The Panzer regimental commander must always keep a reserve of tanks up his sleeve, which he can use at a moment's notice to block any threat from the flank."

A flank shot to the Panther series did not always result in a kill, however. In a wartime report, American tanker Sergeant Francis W. Baker describes such an incident:

> I was tank commander of a Sherman medium tank mounting a 75mm gun. The Germans staged a counterattack with infantry supported by at least three Mark V tanks. Ordering my gunner to fire at the closest tank, which was approximately 800 yards (731 meters) away, he placed one right in the side, which was completely visible to me. To my amazement and disgust, I watched the shell bounce off the side. My gunner fired at least six more rounds at the turret and track. I

> was completely surprised to see it moving after receiving seven hits from my gun.

One of the positive points about the design of the Panther tank that came out of *Operation Zitadelle*, proven over and over again in subsequent operations, was the fact that the frontal armor on the Panther turret and hull could resist penetration by most Allied antitank weapons, except at very close ranges. A 1944 British army report confirming the effectiveness of the frontal armor on the Panther read, "While the armor of the Panther is less thick than that of the Tiger, the use of sloped plates at high angles gives it a very good degree of protection. The hull front is immune to 6-pounder (57mm gun) at all ranges and can only be defeated by the 17-pounder (76.2mm gun) under very restricted conditions."

All of the principal joints in the Panther tank's armor plates were interlocked as well as welded together. An interlocking armor-plate design reduces the amount of welding as compared with a full-penetration joint. Excessive heat applied to the armor plate weakens the material and lowers its effectiveness. Interlocking also provides superior mechanical support against projectile impacts from both the front and side, reducing dependence on weld quality. The effectiveness of this method of construction appears in a postwar U.S. Army report describing the results when an M26 Pershing heavy tank

The late-production Panther Ausf. A tank being set in place by a crane truck had resided at the bottom of a Polish river for more than 45 years. The Daimler-Benz–built tank had been in service with the 25th Panzer Division when the crew decided to drive over an ice-covered Polish river in January 1945. The ice was unable to support the weight of the tank, and the vehicle sank into the shallow river. *Michael Green*

After more than two years of work, the late-production Panther Ausf. A tank, formerly of the 25th Panzer Division, begins to once again take shape. Since most of the original turret of the tank suffered irreparable damage in an explosion set by the crew before they abandoned their vehicle, a new turret based on measurements of surviving Panther Ausf. A tank turrets was commissioned. Seen here is the reproduction turret, to which some of the original surviving pieces are being attached. *Michael Green*

fired at the front of a Panther hull as, "90mm APC M82 projectile impacted on the upper hull front plate of a German Panther tank resulted in weld cracking as long as 62 inches [157.5 cm], from a single round. The interlocking design of the joints, however, prevented the displacement of the armor."

For American tank and tank destroyer crews who faced the Panther in battle and survived, the vehicle made a very strong impression on them, as seen in this extract from a wartime interview with Sergeant Thomas P. Welborn of the 2nd Armored Division:

> On August 1944, in the vicinity of St. Sever Calados (St.-Sever Calvados), France, I witnessed a German Mark V tank knock out three M4 [medium tanks] and three M5 [light] tank[s] during and after being hit by at least 15 rounds of APC from a distance of approximately 700 yards (670 meters). All these shells had ricocheted, with the exception of a 16th round, which finally put the Mark V out of action.

THE PANTHER AUSF. A

Production of the replacement for the Panther Ausf. D began in September of 1943. The new Panther Ausf. A (Sd.Kfz. 171) consisted of a Panther Ausf. D chassis fitted with a redesigned turret. By the time production of the Panther Ausf. A ended in May 1944, German industry had produced 2,200 units.

One of the most obvious visual differences between the D and A models of the Panther was the tank commander's cupola on top of the turret. The Panther Ausf. D turret had an armored, drum-shaped cupola about 10 inches (25.4cm) tall. It had six direct-vision slots arranged around the circumference for the vehicle commander to observe outside the tank. The vehicle commander could close the vision slots from within the tank by rotating a steel ring around the exterior of the cupola.

The Panther Ausf. A came with a cast-armor cupola with seven hooded periscopes arranged around the circumference. The improved visibility offered by this arrangement was very popular with the *Panzertruppen*. The cupola on the Panther Ausf. A also had a fixed ring for mounting a 7.92mm machine gun to use against enemy infantry or low-flying enemy aircraft. This feature had first appeared on some production units of the Panther Ausf. D.

Another easily detected visual difference between the Ausf. D and mid- production Ausf. A Panthers appeared in late 1943. It consisted of an armored spherical-bow machine gun mount in the right-hand corner of the vehicle's front armored plate (called the glacis by tankers) through which a 7.92mm machine gun fired. Aiming, firing, and loading of the machine gun became the duty of the Panther tank radioman. Since the new machine gun position incorporated a self-contained sighting device, the builders of the Panther Ausf. A deleted the fixed forward-looking radioman's periscope seen on the Ausf. D and earlier Ausf. A Panther tanks. British army examinations of captured Panther tanks led them to conclude that the angle of view through the small sighting device in the ball machine gun mount was inadequate, and that it was a mistake by the Germans to have done away with the radioman's forward-facing periscope on the later production units of the Ausf. A.

Prior to the appearance of the spherical-bow machine gun position on late-production Panther Ausf. As, the radioman's vision on all Panther Ausf. Ds and early-production Panther Ausf. As was restricted to a small rectangular observation slot in the right corner of the glacis. When the observation slot was not in use, the radioman covered it with a hinged armored hatch cover. If required, the radioman could fire a 7.92mm machine gun stored within the tank from the open observation slot and direct the weapon's fire by using his overhead periscope.

The Ausf. letter designations for the different versions of the Panther tank meant very little to the *Panzertruppen*. All versions of the Panther were expected to perform the same mission roles. It was only necessary to know the specific Ausf. type when ordering spare parts. The manufacturers, of course, kept detailed records of version and variations for each vehicle produced.

Beginning with Panther Ausf. A tanks built in late 1943, the three small pistol ports with plugs, called *MP Stopfen*, located on the sides and rear of the turret, were replaced by a grenade launcher, called the *Nahverteidigungswaffe* (close-defense weapon) over the loader's position. It could fire anti-personnel grenades, smoke grenades, and signal flares. While the *Nahverteidigungswaffe* could be traversed 360 degrees by the loader, its elevation was fixed at 50 degrees. Due to a shortage of the devices early in production, the opening on some Panther Ausf. As was covered by a bolt-on plate.

PANTHER G

The replacement for the Panther Ausf. A was the Panther Ausf. G (Sd.Kfz. 171), consisting of a Panther Ausf. A turret on a newly improved chassis, which included thicker torsion bars to compensate for an increase

This late-production Panther Ausf. A tank is on display at the Musée des Blindés (tank museum) at Saumur, France. It features a spherical ball mount in the glacis plate, which mounts a 7.92mm machine gun operated by the vehicle's radioman. The mount began appearing on the Panther Ausf. A production lines beginning in late 1943, to replace the "letterbox" machine-gun port, a vertical slot with an armored cover. Starting in September 1944, the new-production Panther Ausf. A tanks got an overhead periscope for their loaders. *Ground Power Magazine*

in vehicle weight. Production of the Panther Ausf. G began in the spring of 1944 and ended in April of 1945, as the victorious Allied armies swept through the country, occupying German factories. Captured German documents indicated that at least 2,943 Panther Ausf. Gs made it across the assembly lines before production ceased, making it the most numerous model of the Panther series.

An important spotting feature for the Ausf. G chassis of the Panther series was the single, large, tapering superstructure plates on either side of the vehicle, which replaced the two-piece superstructure plate of previous models. This change came about due to the pressing need to simplify production in order to expedite delivery to the Panzertruppen.

Since the slope on the new, one-piece upper side superstructure side plates on the Panther Ausf. G version was only 29 degrees (versus the 40-degree slope on earlier

A decision to simplify the design of the Panther Ausf. A chassis was made in the summer of 1943. This redesign effort resulted in the introduction of the Panther Ausf. G, consisting of a new, simplified chassis, with the unmodified turret taken from the Panther Ausf. A. This particular Panther Ausf. G was stalked and destroyed by a Canadian soldier armed with a PIAT (Projector, Infantry, Antitank). *George Bradford collection*

versions), a plate thickness of 2 inches (50 millimeters) was required to maintain equivalent density. To avoid exceeding the chassis load limits by the heavier superstructure armor, the thickness of the lower front hull plate was decreased from 2.4 inches (60 millimeters) to 2 inches (50 millimeters), and the forward section of the hull floor was decreased from 1.2 inches (30 millimeters) to 1 inch (25 millimeters).

On the Panther G, the front superstructure roof, in front of the transmission access hatch, was thickened to provide more structural strength for the pivoting periscopes of the driver. Combat experience had demonstrated to the *Panzertruppen* that on many occasions a hit on the upper glacis from a projectile would distort the 0.64-inch (16-millimeter) roof of the vehicle's superstructure and knock the driver's periscope out of alignment.

On very late production examples of the Panther Ausf. G, a design fix appeared aimed at correcting a ballistic weak spot in the tank's armor. A few lucky enemy tankers and antitank gunners had bounced AP projectiles downward into the driver and radioman's stations of the Panther D and A models by striking a point just below the horizontal centerline of the mantlet. Some U.S. Army tankers remember this tactic being explained in training classes on German tanks before the Allied invasion of France on June 6, 1944, best known to most Americans as D-day.

Beginning in September 1944, a new mantlet began appearing on some production Panther Ausf. Gs that featured an armored chin across the bottom of the mantlet. This protrusion deflected incoming rounds away from the vehicle's upper-superstructure hull plate.

MAIN ARMAMENT

Operation Zitadelle had proven the significant advantages of the Panther's 75mm main gun: its long-range accuracy and lethality. Panther gunners had regularly destroyed Red Army T34/76 tanks at ranges as long as 2,188 yards (2,000 meters). On a number of occasions, they engaged and destroyed T34/76 tanks at a phenomenal 3,282 yards (3,000 meters). The official German military designation for the 75mm main gun on the Panther series was the 7.5cm Kw.K. 42 L/70.

At least one Panther tank prototype was built with a shorter L/60 version of the 75mm main gun. However, its performance was judged inadequate, and the production guns were all the longer L/70.

The 75mm main gun mounted on all three models of the Panther had a barrel length of just over 19 feet 2 inches (5.79 meters). A double-baffle muzzle brake diffused muzzle blast and minimized recoil. In contrast, the 76.2mm main gun barrel on the original version of the Russian T34/76 was only half as long and lacked a muzzle brake.

A British army report discussed the Panther-series' main gun:

> The main armament is a 7.5cm Kw.K. 42 gun mounted high in the turret. The gun is semiautomatic, and when the empty cases are ejected, they should hit the deflector shield and drop through the deflector guard into a bin beneath. The deflection shield is fitted with a spring clip, which should grip the base of the case and ensure that it does not rebound but drops squarely into the bin below.

The bin held only five empty cartridge cases. If more than five main gun rounds were fired without emptying the bin, hot cartridge cases would be ejected directly onto the floor of the turret after bouncing off the now full cartridge-case storage bin. The bin did have a flexible metal tube connected to the loader's overhead ventilation fan to help dissipate toxic fumes from the spent cartridges cases in the bin.

It is important to understand that the size of a tank's main-gun round is just one element contributing to the overall lethality of a weapon. The barrel design, materials, and length, and the weapon's integration with other elements of the fire-control system, remain critical design factors. German materials and manufacturing technology were far ahead of the Allies' throughout World War II. This made German tank main guns, such as the 75mm on the Panther, far more potent than Allied guns of equal or much larger size.

The 75mm main gun on the Panther fired one-piece (fixed) ammunition. The loader manually inserted a round into the weapon's breech. The first two production versions of the Panther, the D and A models, carried 79 unprotected main gun rounds; 40 were stored horizontally in racks on either side of the vehicle's superstructure and 36 were stored in vertical racks on the hull floor. Three more main gun rounds were stored horizontally in a bin under the turret floor. British army tests on captured A-model Panthers show that only 69 of the main rounds carried in the vehicle were readily accessible by the loader in combat. The other 16 were accessible only with great difficulty. The final production version of the Panther Ausf. G carried 82 main-gun rounds.

According to a British military report dated December 1944, a captured German tanker stated the following regarding the ammunition of Panther tanks then in service:

> *Standard instructions are that 120 rounds for the 7.5cm gun and 3,500 rounds for each MG (machine gun) should be stowed in the Panther before going into action. It is left to the crew to decide on the proportion of AP and HE shells to be carried; normally the proportion should be 50 percent of each. [The] prisoner of war carried 9,000 rounds of MG ammo for his two MGs. Stowage space is provided for 79 rounds of 7.5 cm ammo. The extra 41 rounds are added by removing the racks from ammo-boxes and by carrying some rounds in the spent cartridge box . . . under the recoil guard. No rounds are carried on the floor.*

As with most other tanks of World War II, the Panther depended on kinetic energy (KE) armor-defeating projectiles to penetrate the armor of enemy tanks. Kinetic

On display at the Tank Museum in Bovington is this Panther Ausf. G. The thin, soft-steel plates on the sides of the superstructure can make it difficult to tell the Ausf. A apart from the Ausf. G version of the Panther tank. However, by looking at the glacis it is much easier to identify a Panther Ausf. G due to the elimination of the driver's front vision port and one of his two overhead periscopes. *Tank Museum–Bovington*

PzKpfw V, Ausf G (SdKfz 171)
"Panther"

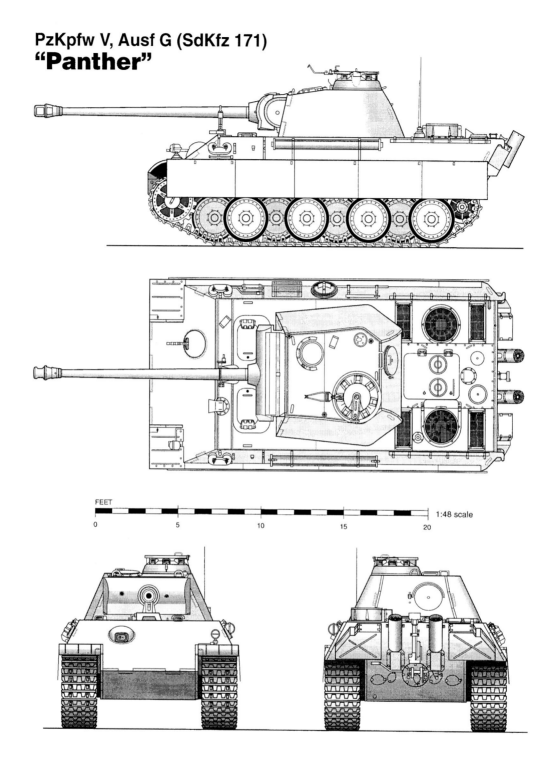

FEET

1:48 scale

0   5   10   15   20

To make up for the deletion of the driver's front vision port and one of the two overhead periscopes on the Panther Ausf. G, the design team for the vehicle provided the driver a single 360-degree rotating overhead periscope. Other changes to the Panther Ausf. G included a new layout on the upper engine deck area and a new muffler arrangement, inherited from the defunct Panther II hull design that never made it into production. *George Bradford*

energy is the product of mass and projectile speed at the time of impact (striking velocity). An effective round also has to be strong enough to survive the impact so it can penetrate the target.

The standard KE armor-piercing round for the Panther's 75mm main gun bore the designation *Panzergranate* 39/42 (*Pzgr.39/42*) and weighed roughly 31 pounds (14.1 kilograms). The projectile portion weighed about 16 pounds (7.3 kilograms). There was also a small, high-explosive element contained within the projectile. The intent was to increase the damage to the interior of a target vehicle after penetration. The velocity of the round was greater than 3,000 feet per second (915 meters per second) when it left the end of the Panther's main gun barrel. This high velocity allowed the round to penetrate up to 4.44 inches (112 millimeters) of armor sloped at 30 degrees at a range of 1,094 yards (1,000 meters). At a range of 2,188 yards (2,000 meters), it could penetrate 3.52 inches (88 millimeters) of armor sloped at 30 degrees.

Author Kerry Erickson has done extensive background research on the Panther tank at various archives in the United States. He describes what American military tests revealed about the performance of the vehicle's main gun:

Accuracy testing conducted at Aberdeen Proving Ground in 1946 showed that, at 1,000 yards (914 meters), the 75mm main gun on the Panther could put all of its shots within a 12-inch (30.5-centimeter) circle. Tests done the year before had demonstrated that the ammunition fired from the Panther had such a flat trajectory that the gunner did not even have to change elevation settings until he began to engage enemy targets at ranges greater than 2,000 yards (1,828 meters).

A German military drawing from World War II shows the interior of a Panther Ausf. D turret. Visible directly under the breech end of the main gun is the hydraulic traversing unit for the turret. Located at the rear of the turret basket floor is a metal bin into which spent cartridge cases would drop once ejected from the breech of the tank's 75mm main gun. *Tank Museum–Bovington*

This picture, taken from the loader's position on the right side of a Panther Ausf. G turret, shows the seats for the vehicle commander and gunner. From his fixed seat, the vehicle commander could obtain all-around vision through the seven periscopes in his overhead cupola. There was also a small folding platform, located directly above the fixed seat, which the commander could stand on, thereby allowing him to raise his head above the cupola. *Michael Green*

This picture taken from the rear of a Panther Ausf. G turret shows the breech end of the 75mm main gun. Missing in this picture is the main gun recoil guard that would have divided the inside of the turret in half. The flexible circular tubing seen on the loader's side of the turret ran from the roof-mounted ventilator down to the metal bin that contained the spent main gun cartridges and helped to remove any leftover propellant gases. *Tank Museum–Bovington*

The Panther's main gun was also capable of firing the *Sprenggranate 42* (*Sprgr.* 42), a high-explosive (HE) round. The round's muzzle velocity of 2,300 feet per second (701.5 meters per second) allowed Panther crews to engage enemy infantry formations well beyond the range of the machine guns. Other potential targets for the *Sprgr.* 42 included towed antitank guns and enemy defensive positions. Most German tankers identified camouflaged and towed enemy antitank guns as more of a threat to them than enemy tanks, since they were harder to spot and typically got in the first shot.

For use against late-war Red Army heavy tanks like the IS-2, Panther crews sometimes used an APCR round designated the *Panzergranate 40/42* (*PzGr.* 40/42). This potent round had a muzzle velocity of 3,672 feet per second

(1,120 meters per second) and could penetrate 6 inches (150 millimeters) of armor sloped at 30 degrees.

A 7.92mm coaxial machine gun was fixed in forward firing position alongside the Panther tank's main gun. Coaxial machine guns traversed and elevated in tandem with the main gun. Their purpose was to engage infantry and lightly armored targets that did not warrant the use of a main gun round. The gunner pressed a foot switch to fire the coaxial machine gun.

TURRET CREW

The tank commander's station for the Panther tank was located toward the rear of the turret on the left side of the main armament. He could either sit on a non-adjustable padded seat fixed to the turret ring or stand on a small platform raised above the floor. Although there was no backrest for the tank commander when seated, he could lean back against the turret in reasonable comfort. When standing on the small platform hinged to the spent-cartridge bin, the tank commander could observe with his head and shoulders outside the turret cupola.

The tank commanders on all three production versions of the Panther tank had access to a scissors-type periscope designated the TSR 1 Sehstab. The periscope was mounted in an adjustable socket close to the front of the cupola. American soldiers who examined captured examples concluded that its purpose was to allow observation of fire by the tank commander without having his view obscured by the effects of muzzle blast and to improve vision from concealed positions. In addition, all three production versions of the Panther had a simple sighting vane mounted to the top of the vehicle turret directly in front of the vehicle commander's cupola. This feature allowed Panther tank commanders to make a rough target indication to their gunners. There were also graduations (labeled 1-12) inside the cupolas of the Panther series to indicate the position of the turret relative to the hull.

The Panther gunner sat on the left side of the turret basket on a padded seat with a backrest. His seat was below and directly in front of the tank commander. His only route for entering or exiting the turret was the tank commander's cupola. He aimed the main gun with a 2.5-power, two-lens binocular sight in the original D version of the Panther tank. Later versions of the Panther Ausf. A and Ausf. G featured a single-lens telescopic sight with dual magnification, with either 2.5-power and a 28-degree field of view or 5-power with 14-degree field of view. A British army report said about the sight: "The gun sight, type TZF12a, is a monocular, and the front end is articulated to move as the gun is elevated. The eyepiece is stationary and comfortable, but badly positioned, since the right earpiece of the gunner's headset must be pushed to one side before he can look through the sight."

The following quote from a German prisoner of war in regards to the gunner's optical sight on the Panther tank appeared in a May 1944 Allied intelligence publication:

Panther personnel . . . are trained to engage a Sherman tank without hesitation at a range of from 2,000 to 2,200 yards (1,828 to 2,429 meters). They are taught that while the preferable range of 800 to 900 yards (731 to 823 meters) will improve accuracy, it will not add greatly to the punch. The gun has an optical sight with three graduations: one for high-explosive shells, one for armor-piercing shells, and the third for the coaxially-mounted machine gun. Each graduation has its own range subdivision.

To fire the Panther's main gun, the gunner pulled a steel lever pivoted to his manually-operated elevation

Looking straight down from the vehicle commander's seat on a Panther Ausf. G turret is the gunner's adjustable padded seat. Visible are the gunner's vertical, manually-operated turret-traverse handwheel on the left and his horizontal, manually-operated elevation handwheel for the main gun, on the right. On the bottom of the turret floor, just in front of the driver's seat, are the two power-operated foot pedals used for traversing the vehicle's turret. *Michael Green*

Looking directly up from the loader's position inside a Panther Ausf. G turret is the vehicle commander's cupola. There are seven 4-inch-wide (100 millimeters) periscopes mounted in the fixed cupola, fitted with rubber brow-pads. The handle visible in the picture opened and closed the pivoted overhead hatch on the cupola. *Michael Green*

handwheel (located to his left), which fired the weapon electrically.

Like all tanks, the Panther had an emergency firing device for the main gun. On the Panther, it was located on the floor below the front edge of the gunner's seat. A British army report described it as the standard German push-button generator type, which was protected by a hinged strip of steel frame that prevented accidental operation.

Since the Panther's main gun lacked any kind of stabilization system, the vehicle had to come to a complete stop before the gunner could engage a target. The only tanks with stabilized guns during World War II were American, and included the M5 Stuart and M24 Chaffee light tank series and the M3 and M4 medium tank series. However, their main guns were stabilized in elevation only. Modern tanks like the American M1 Abrams series have two-axis gun and sight stabilization systems that

dynamically compensate for elevation and traverse while the vehicle is moving.

The Panther Ausf. D came with a single-speed, power turret traverse system, while the Ausf. A and Ausf. G versions of the tank came with a two-speed hydraulic-power turret traverse system, described here in a British army report:

> *The power traverse is hydraulically driven from the [engine] propeller shaft through the two-speed gearbox situated below the gun and on the right of the gunner's seat. Speed and direction of traverse are controlled by two foot pedals, each 3 inches by 4 inches [7.62 centimeters by 10.2 centimeters] on the turret floor in front of the gunner . . . When the left or right pedal is depressed, the turret traverses left or right correspondingly. A linkage is fitted to ensure that the pedal plates remain*

horizontal, as they are depressed . . . In the vehicle inspected, the pedal movement [was] stiff to operate. Considerable foot pressure was required to overcome the inertia, and it was very difficult to start and check the traverse smoothly and at the right moment.

Due to the amount of inertia within the hydraulic turret traverse system, the Panther's gunner took final aim on his chosen target with the tank's manual turret traverse system, which consisted of a 10-inch-diameter, almost horizontal wheel directly in front of the gunner's seat. On the underside of the wheel was a 3-inch-long handle that the gunner rotated to turn the turret. British army tests on Panther tanks showed the manual turret traverse system required little effort, but was very slow.

On the Panther Ausf. D, the maximum turret traverse rate in power mode was 360 degrees in 60 seconds. On the Panther Ausf. A, the turret traverse rate was pushed up to 360 degrees in 15 seconds—four times as fast. However, starting in November of 1943, the factories began governing Panther engines at a lower maximum speed. This change lowered the maximum turret traverse speed to 360 degrees in 18 seconds. The power-operated turret traverse speed on all versions of the M4 Sherman series, except the 105mm howitzer-equipped version, was 15 seconds to rotate the turret 360 degrees.

While some American tankers assumed that the slower power traverse of the Panther series was a tactical disadvantage, a World War II report by a M36 tank destroyer (TD) crew gave a different perspective, saying, "Members of Company A state that, although the Mark V tank has

A captured Panther Ausf. G appears in this photograph. In a U.S. Army report submitted in 1945 by the 2nd Armored Division, an M4 Sherman tank commander recalled, "We saw four Mark Vs at 800 to 1,000 yards in front of us. We opened fire with AP [armor piercing] ammunition and hit them on the right, but our shells ricocheted off. [We fired] about 20 rounds, but did not hurt them in any way, although we hit them consistently." *Patton Museum*

The loader on all the Panther-series tanks entered and exited the vehicle through a circular access hatch in the rear of the vehicle's turret. To help the loader climb in and out of the turret, there were two handles: one on the inside portion of the hatch and another on the top of the rear turret roof. Due to the difficulty in opening and closing the loader's hatch from outside the tank, an additional handle was placed on the outside of the hatch beginning in June 1944. *Thomas Anderson*

a much slower traverse than the M36 [which could rotate its turret 360 degrees in 15 seconds], it has never been their experience that it was not sufficiently fast enough to track any of our tanks, other than the M4 traveling at a very high speed."

A British army report describes the loader's position in the Panther tank as " . . . to the right of the main armament. A seat was optional. As the height of the turret is only 5 feet 3 inches (1.6 meters), a loader of normal height must stoop. The combination of these factors was certain to result in fatigue, especially if the vehicles were on the move for long periods."

The Panther tank's loader entered and exited the turret through an 18-inch-diameter circular hatch located at the rear of the turret. A single overhead fixed periscope provided him with vision over the right front side of the vehicle on Panther Ausf. Ds and Panther Ausf. As built after November/December 1943; earlier versions lacked this periscope.

An electric ventilation fan above the loader's position helped to clear the turret of the fumes given off by spent cartridge cases ejected from the main gun. The top of the ventilator duct projected slightly beyond the top of the turret. In addition, the main-gun breech featured a device that shot a blast of air out the front of the gun tube every time the breech opened to clear out any remaining propellant and the noxious flumes generated by the firing of a main gun round. The American and British military called it a bore evacuator, not to be confused with the bore evacuators of modern tank guns that are mounted on the exterior of the gun tube.

DRIVER'S POSITION

The Panther driver sat at the front left corner of the vehicle's hull. He steered the vehicle with two hydraulically-assisted steering levers positioned on either side of his legs. The gearshift lever was located to the driver's right and provided him with seven forward speeds and a single reverse position. The driver's handbrake was located to his left. The floor-mounted accelerator pedal was on the right, the footbrake was in the center, and the clutch pedal was on the left.

The driver's instrument panel was mounted on the transmission housing to his right. It included a speedometer, tachometer, oil-pressure gauge, and ammeter. To start the vehicle, the driver pushed a starter button on the instrument panel. In very cold weather, or when the Panther tank batteries were too weak to start the engine, the crew could start the engine with an inertia starter located at the rear of the vehicle.

While the padded driver's seat of the D and A models of the Panther tank moved forward and backward, there was no way to adjust their heights. Therefore, the drivers of the Panther Ausf. D and A versions could not operate their vehicles with their heads and upper bodies out of the front superstructure/hull, as U.S. Army tank drivers could. Panther Ausf. D and A drivers normally drove their vehicles by looking through a large, rectangular observation slot, 9 inches (22.9 centimeters) long and about four inches (10.16 centimeters) wide, located directly in front of their seats. The slots contained a laminated glass block to protect them from small-caliber rounds and battlefield fragments. Additional protection for the driver's observation slot came from a hinged armored hatch cover that could be lowered over the vision device from within the confines of the vehicle. Drivers could also view the terrain ahead of their tanks through two overhead fixed periscopes.

On the Panther Ausf. G, the designers did away with the driver's direct-vision observation slot because it was a ballistic weak spot in the frontal armor. They also eliminated the two fixed overhead periscopes on the Panther D and A models. In their place, the Panther Ausf. G featured a single 5-inch-wide (12.7 centimeters) 360-degree rotating and tilting periscope at the driver's position.

At the request of the *Panzertruppen*, Panther Ausf. G drivers received the option of operating their vehicles with their head and shoulders protruding out through their open overhead hatch or with their overhead hatch closed and observing the terrain in front of their vehicles with their rotating periscope. Rather than employ a single, adjustable seat, as found on American tanks, the German designers devised two separate seats for the Panther

Ausf. G's driver station. From a British army report appears this description of the arrangement:

> *The upper seat is positioned by hooking the forward end on to the top of the lower backrest, and the upper backrest onto the turret roof. By adjusting the angle of the lower backrest, the upper seat can be moved forward and backward correspondingly. The arrangement is simple and efficient and allows the upper seat and backrest to be completely removed . . . . The seat and position are comfortable and easily assessable, and the large hatch allows the driver considerable body movement . . . . In both the upper and lower position, the seats are mounted squarely to the controls, and the driver*

232138

This photograph shows the interior of a Panther Ausf. D. Visible are the loader's rear circular turret access hatch, and next to that, the handle employed to open the small pistol port in the rear turret wall. Next to the vehicle commander's position is the small circular door used to talk to people outside the tank. The main gun recoil guard, clearly visible dividing the middle of the turret, has the deflector guard at the rear of it. *Patton Museum*

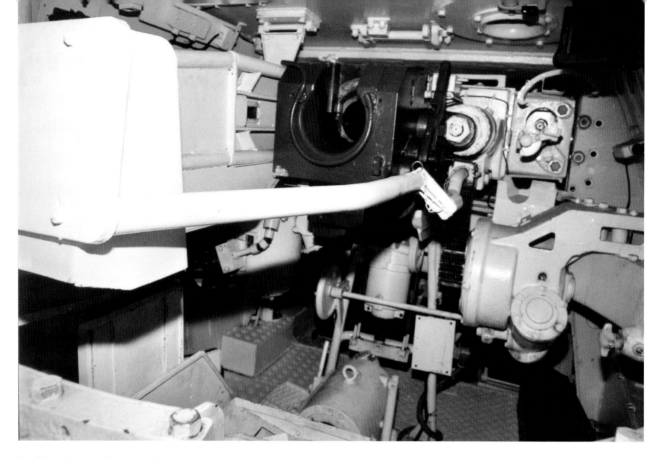

Looking through the loader's rear access hatch on a Panther Ausf. A, one can see the recoil guard that protected the vehicle commander and gunner when the main gun fired. The back end of the deflector guard is visible at the rear of the recoil guard. When the breechblock opened to eject a spent main gun cartridge case, it was supposed to strike the deflector guard and then drop into the empty cartridge-case bin located on the floor of the turret. *Andreas Kirchhoff*

can travel in reasonable comfort when the vehicle is on the move. Although the seats are satisfactory to use, it takes far too long for the driver to change from the upper to lower position. The type of driver's seat fitted in the American 'Pershing' tank is far more suitable.

The two-seat Panther Ausf. G arrangement required the added complexity of adapting or duplicating the driver's controls. When the driver of a Panther G was operating his vehicle from the upper seating position, he operated the 2-foot-long (61 centimeters) steering levers by pulling upwards rather than fore and aft. When operating the vehicle from the lower seating position, the driver repositioned the steering levers by removing a locking pin, rotating the lever around a pivot, and then replacing the locking pin. In this position, the steering levers operated by pulling towards the driver. The gearshift lever for the driver also pivoted for use in both positions.

The handbrake for the Panther Ausf. G driver had separate handles for the two seating positions. The choke control was operable only from the lower seating position. The upper clutch pedal was located about two feet (61 centimeters) above the floor and was rotated out of the way when the driver was in the lower seat. The lower clutch pedal was conventionally mounted on the hull floor. The upper and lower foot brake pedals and accelerator pedals followed the same arrangement as the clutch pedals. There were also separate upper and lower instrument panels.

A U.S. Army report dated January 12, 1945, describing the American soldier's view of the Panther's driving compartment read, "The main criticism that may be made of the driving compartment was that made of the fighting compartment: namely, there is inadequate room for the crew members. The driver is particularly cramped and a large man is at a great disadvantage in trying to operate this vehicle where frequent steering is necessary."

Charles Lemons, curator of the Patton Museum of Cavalry and Armor, sharing his opinion on the comfort level inside a Panther tank, said, "It's a very uncomfortable vehicle. You can sit in a Sherman for at least a day

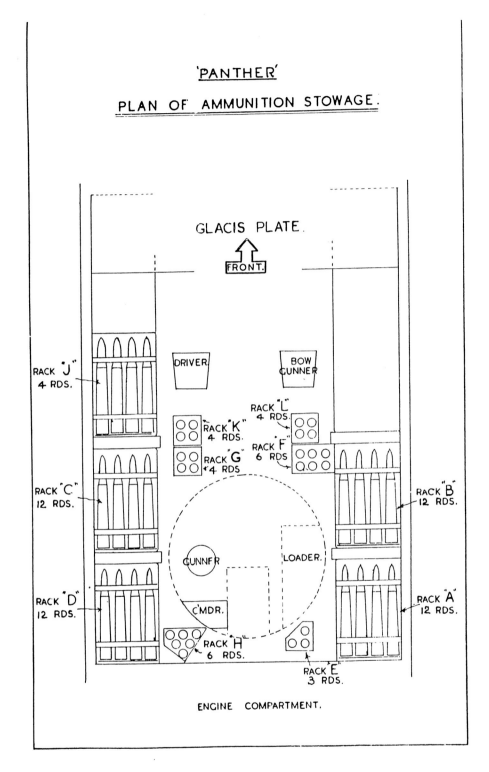

'PANTHER'

PLAN OF AMMUNITION STOWAGE.

GLACIS PLATE.

FRONT.

DRIVER.

BOW GUNNER

RACK "J"
4 RDS.

RACK "L"
4 RDS.

RACK "K"
4 RDS.

RACK "F"
6 RDS.

RACK "G"
4 RDS

RACK "C"
12 RDS.

RACK "B"
12 RDS.

GUNNER

LOADER.

RACK "D"
12 RDS.

RACK "A"
12 RDS.

CMDR.

RACK "H"
6 RDS.

RACK "E"
3 RDS.

ENGINE COMPARTMENT.

This line drawing from a British army report shows the placement of most of the 82 main gun rounds carried inside a Panther Ausf. G tank and the number of rounds stored in each location. There were both vertical and horizontal storage racks in all the various versions of the Panther tank series. Missing from this line drawing are the three main gun rounds stored under the floor of the tank's turret basket. *Tank Museum–Bovington*

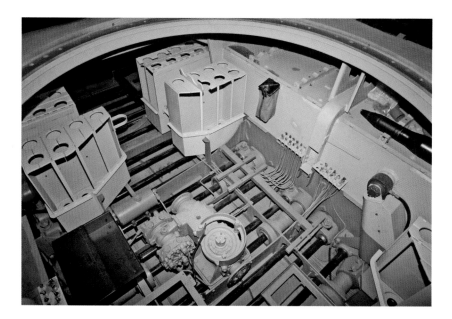

Looking into the hull of the Panther Ausf. A undergoing restoration at the Military Vehicle Technology Foundation, the vehicle's torsion bars and the temporary arrangement of the vertical storage racks can be seen scattered around the bottom of the vehicle's turret basket. Missing in this photo is the diamond-plate flooring. *Michael Green*

or two and not get too uncomfortable, but the Panther . . . . Everything is too small and everything is too close, and it is not easy to get from one place to another within the vehicle. Now, early-model Sherman tanks had the same problem, but they redesigned them."

The driver's and radioman's overhead hatches for the D and A versions of the Panther swung out on a pivot and were held open by small clamps on the top of the hull. Due to their weight, they were very difficult to close quickly. They also jammed quite often. A hatch redesign incorporated into the Panther Ausf. G fitted the hatches with external hinges and counterbalance springs that also served to hold the hatches open without clamps. The downside of this new hatch design was the need for

the vehicle driver and radioman to raise themselves out of their seats to be able to reach over to grasp the handle on the bottom of their overhead hatches to close them. This was a dangerous maneuver in battle conditions.

The German army was not completely happy with the design of the overhead hatches for the driver and radioman. The design of the Panther Ausf. F, which was just entering into production as the war in Europe was ending, featured a brand-new overhead hatch design for the driver and radioman that was very similar to the lift-and-slide design on the Cold War–era U.S. Army M60A1 and M60A3 main battle tanks.

AUTOMOTIVE FEATURES

The Panther synchromesh transmission consisted of two major assemblies: the gear-change mechanism and the steering mechanism. The transmission weighed about

This is a close-up picture of the forward direct-vision port for the driver on the Panther Ausf. D and A. When the port was open, the driver was protected from small-arms fire by a block of replaceable ballistic glass that inserted into the vision port. When heavy fire dictated the driver close his vision port, he lowered the armored flap (seen here) from within the vehicle. *Michael Green*

This nicely restored Panther Ausf. G belongs to the German army technical museum collection (Wehrtechnische Studiensammlung) at Koblenz. The driver is operating the vehicle with his head and upper shoulders protruding out of the overhead hatch. This driving position was used only when action was not imminent and the turret was not likely to turn. *Wehrtechnische Studiensammlung*

3,000 pounds (1,362 kilograms). British military studies of the Panther tank transmission made note of the lavish use of ball-and-roller bearings typical of other German tank transmission designs. They also noticed the extensive lubrication system within the transmission that incorporated oil pipes cast into the gear casing itself.

Analysis of captured Panther tanks and statements made by their crews convinced the British army that the Panther tank transmission entered into production without adequate development and testing. One major flaw was the under-design of the third gear. Designers had apparently expected that the vehicle would not spend much time in third gear. As it turned out, Panther drivers used third gear a great deal. Panther drivers were continually reminded to husband that gear in order to prevent failure on the battlefield. According to a British report, another problem with the transmission design was serious overheating of the gearbox oil in service.

A modern view of the transmission on the Panther tank comes from Jacques Littlefield, president of the Military Vehicle Technology Foundation, which is in the process of restoring a Panther Ausf. A:

It's not badly designed or overly complex the way other systems on the Panther are. It's designed to be compact, efficient, and easy to shift. However, it is certainly not designed for maintenance in the field, as many of the bearings are individually sized for the particular shafts of any one transmission and cannot be interchanged with other Panther transmissions. It was definitely designed by an experienced team and had a lower manufacturing cost and higher reliability than the more complicated pre-select transmissions, as found on many German half-tracks and the Tiger I tank. It is conceptually equivalent to a modern six-speed synchronized transmission, with the big difference being that it was designed for lower speeds and higher torque, with plentiful oil cooling and larger bearings and gears.

The steering unit that formed part of the transmission was a double-differential type, with auxiliary skid brakes. Based on British military observations, the radius of turn in the various gears proved surprisingly large, and, in

An American soldier looks over an abandoned Panther Ausf. G tank, which has its turret traversed rearward. Visible on this tank turret is the very distinctive thickened, squared-off lower portion of the mantlet that began appearing on some Panther Ausf. G tanks late in the war. It was designed to deflect projectiles that struck the bottom of the mantlet and keep them from being directed downward into the upper superstructure. *National Archives*

their opinion, would result in Panther drivers making excessive use of skid steering. The designers of the Panther had provided the vehicle with a neutral-turn ability, allowing it to pivot around its own axis. In a wartime report, an American tanker observed of the Panther tank, "It has, to our minds, greater maneuverability to turn in the space it's sitting in, while our mediums require half a field." The American M4 Sherman medium-tank series used a much simpler controlled-differential steering system that made it impossible to make a pivot turn. Typically, the minimum turn radius of the M4 was anywhere from 30 feet to 80 feet (9.15 to 24.4 meters), depending on the terrain. The Soviet T34/76 medium tank employed a clutch-and-brake steering unit that allowed pivot turns at very low speeds; however, at higher speeds the steering system could cause problems for inexperienced drivers.

Soon after the introduction of the Panther Ausf. D into service, the steering unit exhibited reliability problems. After the war, German tank designers told their British captors that they were well aware of this defect. Their defense of the steering unit design was based on the belief that the steering brakes would outlast a vehicle's transmission and final drives. Hence, it was not the serious problem to the Germans that the British portrayed in their report.

During World War II, a German prisoner of war informed his British captors that the weakness of the Panther's steering mechanism was well known. Panther tank drivers were instructed to use the auxiliary skid brakes for steering and to avoid pivot steers. He went on to say the steering unit problem appeared to be result of the overloading of the steering clutch during tight-radius and pivot steering maneuvers.

A late-war U.S. Army report noted of the Panther's auxiliary skid brake steering ability, "The skid turn feature of the steering system, which is utilized by pulling the steering lever all the way [back] and locking one track, cannot be employed at speeds in excess of approximately 8 to 10 miles per hour (12.9 to 16.1 kilometers per hour), and can only be used when the vehicle is in second gear, as the engine will be stalled if such a turn is made in a higher gear."

British engineers concluded that Panther final-drive units had inadequate bearings and poor housing strength. In addition, critical areas of some gears were not hardened properly. These and other major design and manufacturing defects led to poor final-drive reliability. Later information revealed that the Germans had approached a French firm during the war years to investigate the practicality of producing a new type of final drive for the Panther tank. The French received the assembly drawings, but nothing ever came of the proposed project.

Jacques Littlefield talked about what he has learned about Panther tank final drives in the process of restoring a Panther Auf. A:

My understanding is that the final drives were always a problem. I've heard different things, for instance, that [the Germans] couldn't get the proper alloy, they couldn't heat-treat it properly, or whatever. When we tested ours, the alloy and the strength of these particular gears was as good as what we could make them from today. [We] looked at maybe duplicating them, using the same physical size, but just using a stronger alloy or better treatment, and the answer we got back was that it was as good then as we can do it now.

Part of the problem with the final drives was no doubt due to the vehicle's growth in weight. It grew in weight from its original goal of 30 to 35 tons [27 to 32 metric tons] to the low 40s [36.3 metric tons]. I'm going to guess that what ended up happening with the final drives is that they were designed for the lower-weight vehicle, and there wasn't the physical size [available] to where you could make the gears wider and stronger. Since they weren't able to make them wider, they just left them the way they were originally designed.

It is interesting that the American Sherman tank used double-herringbone gears in the final drives, which provides more torque capability for a given width of a final drive. The Panther uses straight spur gears, so there must have been a manufacturing limitation, as double-herringbone gears were well known at the time for their ability to carry larger amounts of torque for a given width.

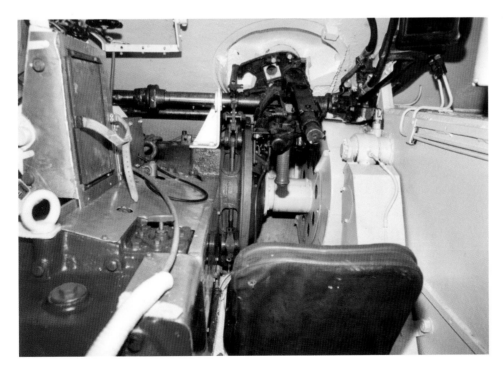

This picture shows the radioman's position in the Panther Ausf. A tank that belongs to the collection of the Deutsches Panzermuseum. The padded seat for the radioman allows for both forward and backward adjustment of the seat in six different positions. While British army tests of the Panther tank showed the radioman's seat to be comfortable, the position is not easily accessible, despite the large overhead hatch provided. *Andreas Kirchhoff.*

This close-up picture of a Panther Ausf. A tank undergoing restoration at the Military Vehicle Technology Foundation shows the receiver end of the 7.92mm machine gun located at the radioman's position. The sight for the weapon is on the left side of the receiver. The lampshade-like device attached to the weapon fitted to the top of the radioman's head and allowed him to move the weapon in its mount when firing. *Michael Green*

ENGINE

From information gleaned by inspecting Panther Ausf. Ds captured in the summer of 1943, the Russians told the British army that two different engine types were used in the German tanks. Early production Panthers were fitted with the same 650-horsepower water-cooled HL 210 Maybach gasoline engines found in early Tiger I heavy tanks. The more common Panther tank power plant consisted of a water-cooled Maybach HL 230 P30 gasoline engine that produced 700 horsepower. The builders of the Panther Ausf. D made the switch to the more powerful engine with the 250th Panther Ausf. D built.

The Maybach HL 230 P30 gasoline engine gave the Panther a top speed of about 30 miles per hour (48 kilometers per hour). The top speed was used primarily for road marches. The average operational speed was typically 15 miles per hour (24 kilometers per hour). The fuel tanks at the rear held 165 gallons (624 liters) of gasoline, which gave the Panther a maximum radius of action on roads of roughly 100 miles (161 kilometers). Traveling off-road dramatically reduces the radius of action of any vehicle.

A serious problem with the Panther-series engine was its propensity to spontaneously burst into flames. Shortly after World War II, the British military tested a number of Panther Ausf. G tanks on their cross-country mobility courses. The test report noted, "Engine compartment fires occurred in each of the four vehicles involved in the trial, in the majority of cases more than once. The fires

In this exterior view of the ball mounting for the radioman's 7.92mm machine gun on the Panther Ausf. A tank belonging to the Military Vehicle Technology Foundation one can see the small opening for the weapon's sight. On the American M4 Sherman tank, the bow-gunner in the front hull had no sight for his .30-caliber Browning machine gun. Instead, he would use his periscope to watch the direction of his tracer rounds to guide his aim onto a target. *Michael Green*

generally started in the vicinity of the carburetors and had been attributed to a tendency for carburetor flooding, the actual conflagration breaking out as a result of a backfire." Charles Lemons, Patton Museum curator, amplified on the problems the Panther tank's proclivity to backfire could cause, saying, "The Panther was one of those vehicles that was a very unforgiving vehicle for a novice driver. If you pushed the gas just the wrong time at the wrong place, it would backfire out of the engine and catch fire, and you were basically sitting in a very large target."

What did Panther tank crews think of their vehicle's technical problems? Dr. Wolfgang Sterner, a World War II Panther tank commander, answered:

I experienced some of them (technical problems) when I was assigned to the Panzer Lehr Division in January 1945. However, by then the technical problems with the Panther were not so dramatic anymore, because at that time many things had been improved. Of course, another positive factor was the shorter distances on the Western Front. Therefore, the strain on the mechanical equipment of a tank was not as severe as [it] would be on the Eastern Front. We still had technical breakdowns with the Panther, but not much more than with the Mark IV. On the other hand, we never had any problems with the tactical fighting capabilities of the Panther; in my opinion it was outstanding.

Being driven around the grounds of the Tank Museum in Bovington in the summer of 2004, is the world's only running Tiger I tank. Captured by a British army tank unit in North Africa in April 1943, the tank later arrived in England for technical evaluation. After the end of World War II, it became an important part of the museum's collection. *Tank Museum–Bovington*

On roadside display in the small Belgian town of La Gleize is this Tiger B with the Henschel-designed turret. Notice how the turret lacks the protrusion for the vehicle commander's position that is so noticeable on the Porsche-designed Tiger B turrets. *Andreas Kirchoff*

CHAPTER FOUR
HEAVY TANKS

THE GROUNDWORK OF WHAT WOULD later become the Tiger I heavy tank began in May 1941 with a set of design specifications issued by the German army ordnance department. The specifications for the new heavy tank, originally designated the VK 45.01, called for a heavily armored vehicle weighing up to 45 tons (40.8 metric tons) and armed with a modified version of an existing dual-purpose, high-velocity gun designated the 8.8cm Flak 36. Allied soldiers of World War II best knew this weapon as the "88." The term "flak" is a German abbreviation for *Flugabwehrkanone*, which in English means antiaircraft gun.

The German army invited Porsche and Henschel & Sons to design the VK 45.01. They were required to have the first prototype of their respective vehicles ready for inspection on Hitler's birthday, April 20, 1942. The German military invasion of the Soviet Union a few weeks later and the discovery that the Red Army T34/76 medium tank was far superior to existing German tank designs only hastened the two firms' desire to quickly field a production version of the VK 45.01 in order to restore the battlefield superiority of the *Panzertruppen*.

Dr. Ferdinand Porsche was a close confidant of Hitler and was convinced that the winning contract would go to his firm. However, the German army's evaluation of the competing heavy-tank designs, done over a two-month period, clearly showed that the Henschel entry was superior in almost every aspect. A major defect of the Porsche design was its inferior reliability. Full-rate production of the Henschel heavy-tank design, now designated the Pz.Kpfw. VI Ausf. H (Sd.Kfz. 182), began in August of 1942.

During the development process, the Henschel heavy tank design had grown in weight, a common occurrence for tank designs. The production configuration was more than 10 tons (9.1 metric tons) over the maximum specified weight of 45 tons (40.8 metric tons). The German army accepted the higher weight in exchange for the vehicle's superior armor protection levels and firepower.

TIGER I DESCRIPTION

Both the American and British armies had an abiding interest in German tank development during most of

Prior to restoring the Tiger I in the Tank Museum–Bovington to running condition, the staff disassembled the vehicle and then rebuilt it almost from the ground up. This picture shows the tank's large, box-like hull, minus its turret, and stripped bare of just about anything removable. *Tank Museum–Bovington*

World War II, and they took every opportunity to study captured vehicles. This helped them to identify any weaknesses that tankers and antitank gun crews might exploit in combat. Such research also sometimes helped the Allied armies to keep up with design trends in German tank development and allowed them to develop suitable countermeasures.

The June 1943 issue of the Allied publication *Intelligence Bulletin* described a Tiger I tank captured by the British and Americans in North Africa:

> *In Tunisia, the German army sent into combat—apparently for the first time [Note: The actual first use was on the Russian front in late 1942.]—its new heavy tank, the Pz.Kw. VI, which it calls the 'Tiger'. The new tank's most notable features are its 88mm gun, 4-inch (100-millimeter) frontal armor, great weight, and lack of spaced armor. Although the Pz.Kw. VI has probably been adopted as a standard German tank, future modifications may be expected.*
>
> *The Tiger tank, which is larger and more powerful than the Pz.Kw. IV, is about 20 feet (6.1 meters) long, 12 feet wide (3.7 meters) wide, and 9 1/2 feet (2.9 meters) high. The barrel of the 88mm gun overhangs the nose by almost 7 feet (2.13 meters). The tank weighs 56 tons (50.8 metric tons) in action . . . and is reported to have a maximum speed of about 20 miles per hour (32.2 kilometers per hour). It normally has a crew of five (tank commander, gunner, loader, driver, and radioman).*
>
> *The armament of the Pz.Kw. VI consists of the 88mm tank gun (Kw.K. 36), which fires fixed ammunition similar to, or identical to, ammunition for the usual 88mm antiaircraft-antitank gun; a 7.92mm (0.32-inch) machine gun (MG 34) which is mounted coaxially on the left side of the 88mm; and a second 7.92mm machine gun (MG 34) which is hull-mounted and fires forward. In addition, a set of three smoke-generator dischargers is carried on each side of the turret.*
>
> *The tank is provided with two tracks, a wide one (2 feet, 4.5 inches) [72.4 centimeters] and a narrow one (just under 2 feet) [61 centimeters]. The wide track is the one used in battle, the narrow being for administrative marches and where maneuverability and economy of operation take precedence over ground pressure.*
>
> *The angular (as opposed to rounded) arrangement of most of the armor is a bad design feature; reliance seems to be placed on the quality and thickness of the armor, with no effort having been made to present difficult angles of impact. In addition, none of the armor is face-hardened. The familiar German practice of increasing a tank's frontal armor at the expense of the side armor is also apparent in the case of the Pz.Kw. VI.*

The Tiger I tank's hull and superstructure consisted of flat armor plates joined by interlocking stepped welded joints. A description of the turret mantlet on the Tiger I appeared in a British military report dated November 1943 reading: "The cast front plate of the gun mantlet has

Pz Kpfw 'TIGER I' Ausf. E (initial prototypes)

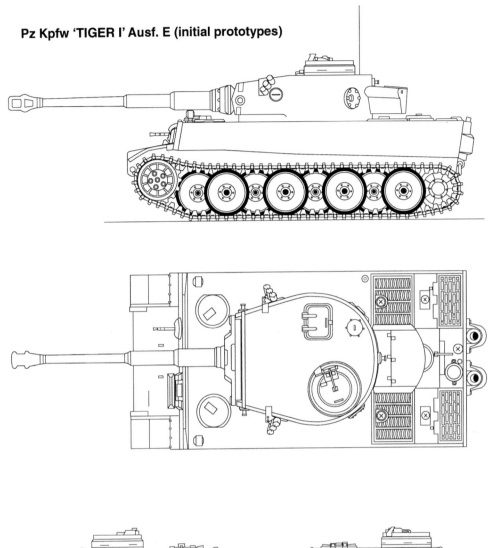

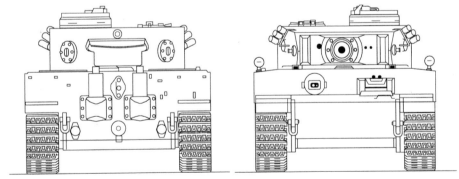

This line drawing illustrates the various external features of one of three experimental Tiger I prototypes. One of the three prototypes appeared before Hitler for his inspection on his birthday—April 20, 1942. None of the prototype Tiger I tanks would ever leave Germany. Instead, they became training vehicles for the newly-formed Tiger I tank units. *George Bradford*

Pz Kpfw 'TIGER I' Ausf. E (early production)

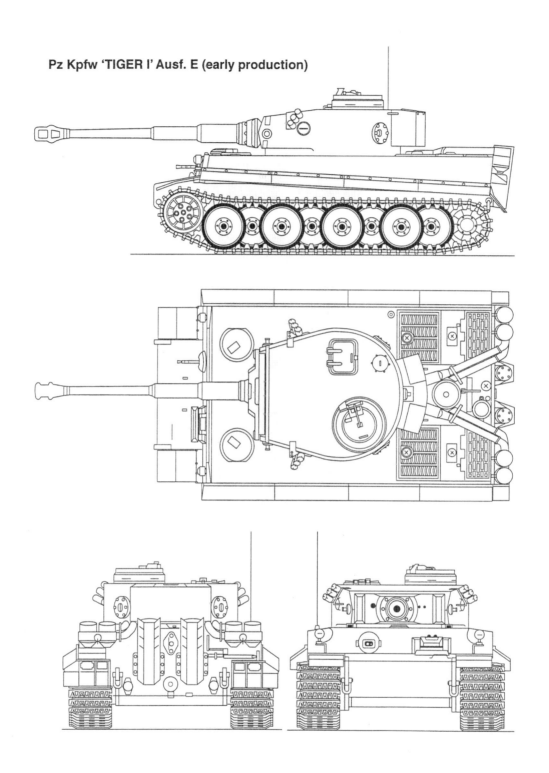

The early-production Tiger I tanks had a variety of exterior characteristics that distinguished them from mid- and late-production versions of the vehicle. For example, the early tanks had a drum-type vehicle commander's cupola, and the aperture for the main gun's binocular telescope was flush with the mantlet, not thickened as those on mid-production vehicles and beyond. The early versions also lacked the loader's rear access hatch in the back of the turret. *George Bradford*

A unit of Tiger I tanks is hitching a ride to the front on a train. The vehicle in the foreground has the early-style drum-like vehicle commander's cupola. To save wear and tear on the tracks and powertrain of its inventory of Tiger tanks, the German military made every effort to ship them by rail as close to the battlefield as possible. *Patton Museum*

a thickness of 92mm (3.68 inches) over the full height and breadth. Measured through the gun sight borings, the thickness is 100mm (4 inches). In the centre portion where the front plate is reinforced around the gun, the thickness is increased to 200mm (8 inches). There is no spaced armor or the provision for the fitting of it."

The Tiger I tank's turret, which appeared horseshoe-shaped in plan view, was made from a single 3.28-inch-thick (82 millimeters) armor plate joined to a point just behind the tank's mantlet. The vehicle's massive turret normally rotated with the aid of a hydraulic-power traverse system driven by the tank's engine. The Tiger tank gunner used his manual elevation and traversing controls for the final laying (aiming) on a selected target or as a backup in case the power traverse system was off.

The superstructure's front vertical armor plate on the Tiger I tank was 4.1 inches (102 millimeters) thick and sloped at an angle of only 10 degrees. Located directly below that plate, the glacis plate was sloped at 80 degrees and was 2.44 inches (61 millimeters) thick. Just below the glacis plate, the front hull-nose plate was 4.08 inches (102 millimeters) thick and sloped at 24 degrees.

The roof on the Tiger I tank turret was only 1.04 inches (26 millimeters) thick, as was the top of the front and rear superstructure and the bottom of the tank's hull. Side superstructure armor thickness on the Tiger I was 3.2 inches (80 millimeters) at 0 degrees, with the lower hull side plates being 2.52 inches (63 millimeters) thick. The rear engine plate on the tank was 3.28 inches (82 millimeters) thick and sloped at 8 degrees.

This mid-production Tiger I is somewhere in Russia in the winter of 1942 or 1943. It can be identified by the large hinge where the loader's rear access hatch is located in the rear of the vehicle's turret, just in front of the stowage bin on the rear of the turret. The crew has whitewashed the tank to aid in its concealment from the enemy. *Patton Museum*

TIGER I TANKS IN COMBAT

The Tiger Primer, a small instructional handbook first published in August 1943, was issued to all Tiger I crewmen. The *Primer*, describing the effectiveness of the vehicle's armor by telling the story of a Tiger I tank that fought in a battle on the Russian front, read, "This Tiger received 227 hits from antitank rifles, 14 hits with a 5.2cm gun, and 11 hits with a 7.6cm gun in 6 hours of fighting. No shot went inside, and the tank made it home on its own power."

Sergeant Harold E. Fulton, a U.S. Army tank gunner, described an engagement with a number of Tiger I tanks in a 1945 wartime report comparing Mark IV and Mark VI Tiger tanks:

We were ordered to engage a column of six Mark VIs of the early model and two Mark IVs. As gunner, I fired 30 rounds from the 75mm gun of our tank. Some were HE, some smoke, and the rest AP. Each time one of the APs hit the tank, you could see them ricocheting two and three hundred feet into the air. Along with my gun firing, there were four more tanks of my platoon, two or three M4 tanks from another company, and two M7s (self-propelled 105mm howitzers) firing at the same column. The range from my tank to the targets *was five to eight hundred yards (457 to 731 meters).*

Two days later, having a chance to inspect these vehicles, we found the Mark IVs with large holes in the front, but of all the Mark VIs there was one penetration in one tank on the back of the turret. The numerous places where the other projectiles hit there was just grooves or penetrations part way through the armor.

Despite its very thick armor, the Tiger I tank was far from being invincible. It was just as vulnerable to hidden antitank guns as were Allied tanks. In North Africa, a small number of Tiger I tanks were sent to support the Afrikakorps in late 1942. They did fairly well against Allied tanks and antitank guns in their initial combat engagements. However, on January 20, 1943, two Tiger I tanks unknowingly passed in front of a British antitank gun position and exposed their thinner side armor to the gunners. A description of that encounter is included in a report filed in the Public Archives of Canada:

The first of the new German heavy tanks to be destroyed in this theatre was accounted for by 6-pounders (57mm) of the Antitank Bn (battalion).

Taken at the Tank Museum, this very interesting picture shows the museum's early-production Tiger I tank, built in February 1943, parked next to the museum's Pz.Kpfw. III Ausf. L, built in 1942. The huge jump in size and firepower the Germans made with the Tiger I tank is very evident in this picture. *Tank Museum–Bovington*

The emplaced 6-pdrs opened fire at an initial range of 680 yards (621 meters). The first round hit the upper side of the tank at very acute angles [sic] and merely nicked the armor. As the tank moved nearer, it turned in such a manner that the third and fourth shots gouged out scallops of armor, the fifth shot went almost through, and the next three rounds penetrated completely and stopped the tank. The first complete penetration was at a range of 600 yards (548 meters), at an angle of impact of 30 degrees from normal, through homogeneous armor 82mm (approximately 3 1/3 inches) thick. Ammunition used was the 57mm AP semi AP solid shot.

While not usually thought of as tank-killing weapons, Allied artillery played an important antitank role in World War II. An article published in a World War II issue of *Soviet Artillery Journal* provided detailed instructions for the use of antitank weapons against the German Tiger tank. The vulnerability of various parts of the tank were described in detail, along with directions for attacking a Tiger tank:

The mobility of tanks depends upon the proper functioning of the suspension parts—sprocket (small driving wheel), idler (small wheel in the rear), wheels, and tracks. All of these parts are

vulnerable to shells of all calibers. A particularly vulnerable part is the sprocket.

Fire armor-piercing shells and HE (high-explosive) shells at the sprocket, the idler, and the tracks. This will stop the tank. Fire at the wheels with HE shells. Also, when attacking a tank, use

A close-up view shows the vehicle commander's cast-armored steel cupola on a Tiger I tank that belongs to the collection of the Musée des Blindés in Saumur. This style of cupola began appearing on new-production Tiger I tanks beginning in July 1943, and is somewhat similar in design to that placed on the Panther A tank. *Frank Schulz*

Two American soldiers pose in front of a destroyed late-production Tiger I tank. The blackened hull and turret indicate that the tank burned, as does the fact that the rear of the vehicle is badly sagging, no doubt due to the heat of the fire weakening the tank's torsion bars. The main gun also appears to have recoiled into the turret without returning to its normal firing position. *Patton Museum*

AT grenades and mines. If movable mines are used, attach three or four of them to a board and draw the board, by means of a cord or cable, into the path of an advancing tank.

There are two armor plates on each side of the tank. The lower plate is partly covered by the wheels. This plate protects the engine and the gasoline tanks, which are located in the rear of the hull, directly beyond and over the two rear wheels.

Fire at the lower plates with armor-piercing shells from 76, 57, and 45mm guns. When the gasoline tanks are hit, the vehicle will be set on fire. Another method of starting a fire within the tank is to pierce the upper plates on the sides of the tank, thus reaching the ammunition compartments and causing an explosion.

IMPROVED TIGER I

Like most tanks, the Tiger I was continually upgraded throughout its production run as shortcomings in its design were discovered during field use. Tiger I production ran from August of 1942 to August of 1944, with 1,350 vehicles being built. Many design changes were also the result of production decisions made at the factory for cost or manufacturing efficiency reasons.

The designation of the Tiger I tank when it entered full production in August 1942 was Pz.Kpfw. VI H (Sd.Kfz. 182). In March 1943, the designation changed to Pz.Kpfw. VI Tiger Ausf. E (Sd.Kfz. 181). This change was merely of nomenclature and did not reflect any particular model type for the Tiger I tank. Date of manufacture was the only way to tell Tiger I models apart. Many early Tigers were rebuilt using parts and subassemblies from various production runs. Within the American and

British military, the Tiger I tank was designated the Mark VI or Pz.Kpfw. VI.

The most noticeable visual features that distinguished the late-production Tiger I tanks from the early ones included the stronger steel-rimmed wheels that replaced the original rubber-rimmed road wheels; the Panther Ausf. G medium tank cast-steel-armor-type commander's cupola equipped with periscopes that replaced the more vulnerable drum-type cupola with vision slots; a new escape/loading hatch located on the right-rear side of the turret; and the replacement of the one-piece diamond-plate mudguards with larger mudguards with extensions that folded down for rail transport. Only the first early-production vehicles had two pistol ports toward the rear of the turret; by February 1943, only the left-hand pistol port was retained.

A NEW TIGER TANK APPEARS

In May of 1941, one month after Hitler saw the first prototypes of the Tiger I tank, the German army approved the design for a new version of the Tiger tank boasting even better armor protection and firepower. The German army again invited Porsche and Henschel to submit detailed designs to meet their needs. As before, the head of Porsche was so confident that his firm had the inside track on the winning of the contract for the next generation Tiger heavy tank that he ordered production

On display near the small French town of Vimoutier is a late-production Tiger I tank that broke down and was destroyed in place by its own crew, to serve as a roadblock, in late 1944. It managed to avoid the scrap dealers after World War II because U.S. Army bulldozers had pushed it into a deep ditch that was difficult to access. Acquired by a local citizen after the war, it now stands as a local tourist attraction. *Lesley Delsing*

By looking down through the vehicle commander's hatch on this Tiger I tank, which belongs to the Musée des Blindés–Saumur, one can see the top of the vehicle commander's manually-operated auxiliary traverse handwheel. It was a feature not found on any other German tanks built before and during World War II, except for the follow-on Tiger B tank. *Frank Schulz*

protruded out over the left side of the turret and created a ballistic weak spot. Because the Henschel turret had a wider roof, its cupola required no such protrusion. The Porsche turret used an electric motor drive to rotate the turret, while the Henschel turret employed a hydraulic-power traverse system, as did the Tiger I and Panther tanks.

The first three pre-production examples of that next-generation Tiger tank came out of the Henschel factory in November of 1943. Full-rate production began in February of 1944. The tank's official designation was Pz.Kpfw. VI Tiger Ausf. B (Sd.Kfz. 182). This designation was normally shortened to just "Tiger B." An unofficial nickname for the tank, first used in a German report dating from January 1945, referred to it as the *Königstiger*

From the vehicle commander's position on a Tiger I tank that belongs to the Musée des Blindés–Saumur, the gunner's seat is visible, minus the seat cushions. At the top of the picture is the gunner's green, horizontal, manually-operated turret-traverse handwheel. Seen at the bottom of the picture is the driver's position, minus the entire seat. *Frank Schulz*

of a Porsche-designed turret and chassis even before the German army had rendered a final decision. Much to the Porsche's dismay, Henschel once again received the production contract from the German army.

Some 80 of the cancelled Porsche-designed chassis later found use as the base upon which a turretless tank destroyer called the *Elefant* was built. About 50 Porsche-designed turrets eventually appeared on the chassis of the winning Henschel heavy tank design. The Porsche-designed turret differed from the Henschel-designed turret in that its sides had greater slope, and it featured a curved front plate and, therefore, turret side plates with convex curves on their front ends. The Henschel-designed turret was a simpler design consisting of a flat front plate and side plates with straight front ends. Another difference between the Porsche and Henschel turret designs was the positioning of their vehicle commander's cupolas. Because the Porsche turret's side plates had greater slope than the Henschel's, its roof was narrower. As a result, the Porsche turret's cupola

This picture, taken from the radio-man's position on a Tiger I tank (looking rearward), shows the two tilting foot pedals, located just below and in front of the gunner's seat, which he used to traverse the vehicle's 20-ton turret hydraulically with power from the tank's engine. The smaller pedal extending out from the metal box upon which the tilting foot pedals are mounted is the gunner's firing device for the tank's coaxial 7.92mm machine gun. *Frank Schulz*

(King Tiger). Within the American and British armies, the Tiger B often went by the name "Tiger II" or "Royal Tiger."

TIGER B DESCRIPTION

The Tiger B weighed almost 75 tons (67.5 metric tons), was 32 feet 8 inches (10 meters) long with its main gun pointed forward, and had a width of 12 feet 3 inches (3.73 meters). It was 10 feet 1 inch (3.07 meters) high. By comparison, the roughly 33-ton (29.7 metric ton) American M4A3 Sherman medium tank was only 20 feet 7 inches (6.27 meters) long with it main gun pointed forward and had a width of 8 feet 9 inches (2.66 meters). The height of the M4A3 was 9 feet 7 inches (2.93 meters).

Power for the Tiger B came from a water-cooled Maybach HL 230 P30 gasoline engine that produced up to 700 horsepower. The U.S. Army captured at least one Tiger B tank with a manual that listed the horsepower rating as only 600. The Americans deduced that the Germans might have done this to increase engine life.

Maximum road speed for the Tiger B was 23.6 miles per hour (38 kilometers per hour) and between 9.3 and 10.4 miles per hour (15–20 kilometers per hour) when traveling off-road. The fuel capacity for the tank was 203 gallons (860 liters), which gave the vehicle a maximum radius of action on roads of 106 miles (170 kilometers) and 74.4 miles (119 kilometers) off-road.

In contrast to the Panther and Tiger I tanks, which had interleaved road wheels, the Tiger B had an overlapping road wheel arrangement consisting of nine wheel arms per side for five outer and four inner road wheels. Each wheel arm connected through a torsion bar, which fitted into a pressure-lubricated housing. At the front of the tank's hull were the driving sprockets, with the idlers at the rear of the hull. While the overlapping wheel arrangement was an improvement over the earlier interleaved road wheel system, it placed a potentially damaging twisting load on the tank's tracks. The interleaved and overlapping road wheel arrangements are heavier than the double road wheels found on the U.S. Army M18 Tank Destroyer or M26 Pershing heavy tank during World War II, as well as all post World War II American and German tanks. Because of these problems, this wheel arrangement has never been used on any other countries' post–World War II series production tanks.

The standard steel tracks upon which the Tiger B tank's road wheels rode were 31 1/2 inches (80 centimeters) wide. There was also a second set of narrower transport tracks available for the Tiger B when transported by rail that were only 26 inches (66 centimeters) wide.

The Tiger B tank could ford a water obstacle up to a depth of 5 feet 9 inches (1.8 meters) without prior preparation. It could climb over a vertical step almost 3 feet (91.4 centimeters) high and drive up a maximum gradient of 35 degrees.

This close-up picture shows the gunner's manually-operated turret-traverse handwheel on this Tiger I tank which belongs to the Musée des Blindés–Saumur. Just above the handwheel is the mounting bracket for the gunner's binocular telescopic sight (not seen here). Later-production Tiger I tanks featured a single-lens optical sight for the gunner. *Frank Schulz*

TIGER B CREW POSITIONS

The five members of the Tiger B crew consisted of the tank commander, gunner, and loader in the turret, and the driver and radio operator in the front hull.

The tank commander's position on the Tiger B, as with the Panther and Tiger I tanks, was in the left rear quarter of the vehicle's turret. He could sit on a padded saddle-shaped seat mounted on a hinged arm attached to the turret wall that could be stowed against it when not required. The curved padded backrest for the tank commander's seat could also be stowed against the turret wall when not in use. From the seated position, the Tiger B tank commander could look in reasonable comfort through any of the periscopes mounted in his overhead fixed cupola. When the tank commander wished to look out over the top of his cupola, he stood on a pair of footrests.

The gunner for the Tiger B tank sat below and directly in front of the tank commander's position on a non-adjustable padded saddle-shaped seat. The curved backrest for the gunner's seat lifted on a hinge on its right side to allow him greater access to his seat. The handwheel for elevating and depressing the tank's main gun was mounted in a vertical plane to the right of the gunner's seat and was air assisted, which, according to Charles Lemon, curator of the Patton Museum of Cavalry and Armor, "when it is operational, you can take two fingers and elevate that gun up and down."

The Tiger B gunner's manually-operated turret traverse handwheel was located between the gunner's knees and was adjustable forward and backward through an arc and could be locked in the desired position. British army tests on captured Tiger B tanks found the gunner's turret-traverse handwheel very unsatisfactory because it was uncomfortable to use.

Normally the gunner on the Tiger B tank would traverse his turret with a hydraulically-operated system driven by the engine propeller shaft through a two-speed gearbox, which was situated below the gun and on the right of the gunner's seat. As with the Panther and Tiger I tanks, the Tiger B gunner could control the direction of the turret and the speed at which it turned by using two foot-operated tilting plate pedals directly in front and below his seat. But the gunner on the Tiger B tank could also control the direction and speed of his turret with a simple plain steel bar mounted on the left side of his seat on the same linkage as the foot-operated tilting plate pedals. By moving it forward, the turret traversed left, while moving it backwards traversed the turret right. British Army tests on captured examples of the Tiger B showed that the two turret-traversing systems could be used either independently or, as was more likely, in unison. With the highest engine speed, the gunner on the Tiger B could traverse his tank's turret 360 degrees in just 19 seconds. With a much lower engine speed it took the gunner 77 seconds to perform a full rotation.

This manually-operated elevation handwheel is located directly below the breech end of the 88mm main gun mounted in the Tiger I turret and to the right of the gunner's seat. The main gun could be elevated 17 degrees and depressed 6.5 degrees by the Tiger I tank gunner. The vehicle commander lacked the ability to raise or lower the main gun from his position, but he could traverse it. *Frank Schulz*

The loader's position in the Tiger B was to the right of the main gun. Like the tank commander, the loader could sit on a padded saddle-shaped seat that folded upward when not needed. A British army report describes the loader's position on a Tiger B tank:

> *The loader has ample space for handling ammunition on his side of the turret. In addition, if the [overhead] hatch is open, a loader whose height is 5 feet 7 inches (174 centimeters) or less can stand erect with his head not touching the turret roof. However, when the hatch is closed, the fittings on the inside of the door project about three inches (7.6 centimeters) below the level of the roof. Since the loader would probably strike his head against them while loading, he would probably keep the hatch open when loading.*

Located just in front of the loader's seat was an auxiliary turret-traverse handwheel, which allowed him to assist the gunner in traversing the tank's turret when the power traverse system was down. The loader had a single

overhead periscope located in front of his rectangular overhead hatch, that was identical to that found on the Tiger I.

There was a rear-turret escape hatch, which hinged downward on the Tiger B. British army tests on captured Tiger B tanks showed that when the vehicle was carrying a full load of main gun rounds in the rear of the turret, it would be impossible for any of the tank's turret crew to leave the vehicle by that route. Even with no main gun rounds stored in the rear of the tank's turret, the British concluded that only a very skinny tanker could fit past the ammunition racks and successfully leave the vehicle's turret by the rear escape hatch.

Visible in this picture taken from the vehicle commander's position on a Tiger I tank is the breech mechanism for the main gun. A breech mechanism is a mechanical opening-and-closing device located at the rear end of the gun tube, which provides entry and sealing of the ammunition in the weapon. At the center of the breech mechanism is the attached firing mechanism, which detonates the ammunition. *Frank Schulz*

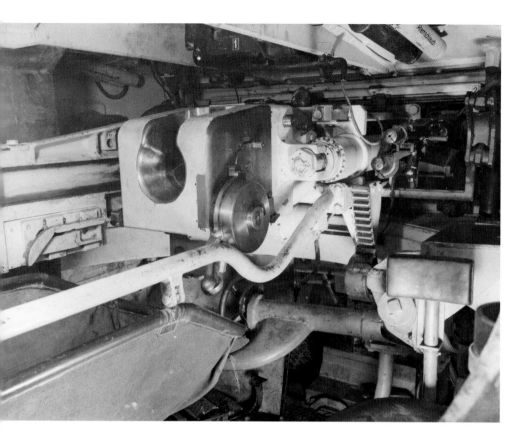

The driver for the Tiger B sat on an adjustable padded seat in the front left quarter of the hull, which allowed him to drive closed-down or opened-up with his head and shoulders outside his overhead hatch. The padded backrest for the driver's seat was also adjustable with a cam, which locked with a lever on the right side of his seat. Since the driver's seat was adjustable for both an upper and lower positions, his controls were accessible in either position. Vision for the driver when closed-down came from an overhead 360 degree rotating and tilting periscope, like those fitted on Panther Ausf. Gs.

The Tiger B driver steered his vehicle with a power-assisted semi-circular steering wheel that raised or lowered to suit his needs. The steering wheel column was telescopic and extended through a range of 11 inches (28 centimeters). When the power steering was not running on the Tiger B tank (i.e. when towed), the driver manually steered his vehicle with standard steering levers mounted on the hull floor. The manual steering levers were accessible only when the driver was in the lower closed-down position.

The Tiger B's front-hull mounted transmission was located in between the driver's and the radioman's position. A description of the transmission appeared in a British Army report:

> The pre-selective gearbox gives eight forward and four reverse ratios. The control lever is a short rod with a knob at the top end and is mounted in a semi-circular 'gate' on top of the gearbox on the right of the driver, who does not have to use the clutch pedal when changing gear, and who has no need to 'rev-up' when changing down. Both of these operations are performed automatically by the gearbox, the clutch pedal being used only for engaging a gear before the tank moves off.

The radioman's position on the Tiger B is described by Charles Lemon, curator of the Patton Museum of Cavalry and Armor:

> The radio operator's seat is basically a pad sitting almost on the deck. It sits on a little box-like structure and there is a folding backrest for it . . . the radio racks sit between the operator and the driver, directly over the final drive and

transmission. The machine gun mount and a large circle around the mount base is painted black. The radio mounts are gray, with the cabling being unpainted steel wire mesh covered. To the radio-operator's right is main gun ammunition storage with a small double rack for spare periscope heads mounted on the lower wall. There is also a storage rack for two machine gun carriers . . . Under the deck, just behind the radio operator's seat are the mounts for the radio power supplies and dynamotors. There is no machine gun ammunition storage in the radio operator's position; all of the ammo bags being stored in racks around the turret ring base or on the crossbeam just forward of the turret.

The circular access hatch mounted in the rear turret wall of a Tiger I tank. Hinged on the outside of the tank's turret, the rear access hatch dropped down flat when opened. It replaced a smaller pistol-firing port seen on early-production Tiger I tanks. The device hanging down from the turret roof is a breech-loaded grenade launcher called the *Nahverteidigungswaffe* (close-defense weapon) that was capable of firing anti-personnel and smoke grenades. *Frank Schulz*

Besides operating the Tiger B's radio sets, the radio operator was responsible for aiming and firing the 7.92mm machine gun mounted in the front superstructure plate in an armored ball mounted as seen on the Panther Ausf. A and Ausf. G. In addition to the optical sight mounted alongside the machine gun, the radio operator had a single fixed overhead periscope.

TIGER B ARMOR PROTECTION

Unlike the Tiger I with its flat, box-like armored shape, the first prototype of the Tiger B featured armor with much more of a slope. This followed in the footsteps of the Panther medium tank, which had in turn been copied from the Red Army's T-34 medium tank. The T-34 owed much of its design to the pre-war tanks of the American designer J. Walter Christie.

From the rear of the loader's position on the Musée des Blindés–Saumur's Tiger I tank is this view of the front of the turret. Visible alongside the breech of the tank's main gun is the mounting bracket for the coaxial 7.92mm machine (not fitted in this vehicle). Also visible is the supporting bracket for the main gun elevation mechanism, attached to the turret wall. *Frank Schulz*

The turret front plate on the Tiger B with the Henschel-designed turret was 7.2 inches (180 millimeters) thick and sloped at an angle of 10 degrees, while the sides of the turret and its rear were 3.2 inches (80 millimeters) thick and sloped at an angle of 21 degrees. The slightly curved turret roof on the tank was 1.6 inches (40 millimeters) thick and sloped at an angle of between 78 to 90 degrees. A description of the mantlet on the Henschel-designed turret appears in a British army wartime report:

> The mantlet design is unusual and is one of the most interesting features of the tank. It represents a distinct departure from previous German practice and is worthy of special consideration. The immunity should be of a very high standard, and particular attention seems to have been given to the design in order to avoid deflection of hits from the mantlet into the hull roof. It would be difficult to jam the mantlet under attack, other than by penetration or at least near-penetration, and because of the bell-shaped casting, such a hit would be difficult to obtain.

The front glacis plate on the Tiger B was 6 inches (150 millimeters) thick and sloped at an angle of 50 degrees, while the superstructure sides were 3.2 inches (80 millimeters) thick and sloped at an angle of 25 degrees. The lower hull armor on the tank consisted of 3.2-inch-thick (80 millimeters) plates, which had no slope. The rear hull plate was 3.2 inches (80 millimeters) thick and sloped at an angle of 30 degrees. The flat roof of the vehicle's superstructure was 1.6 inches (40 millimeters) thick.

In a wartime report, Sergeant Clyde D. Brunson, a tank commander in the 2nd Armored Division, remarked on the effectiveness of the thick, sloped frontal armor:

> One day a Royal Tiger tank got within 150 yards (137 meters) of my tank and knocked me out. Five of our tanks opened up on him from ranges of 200 to 600 yards (183 to 548 meters) and got five or six hits on the front of the Tiger. They all just glanced off, and the Tiger backed off and got away. If we had a tank like the Tiger, we would all be home today.

It usually fell to the U.S. Army's M4 Sherman medium tanks to battle it out with the German Tiger tanks, even though they were not originally designed for that work because specialized tank destroyers were originally assigned that role. Unfortunately, the Sherman's standard M61 armor-piercing round for its 75mm gun just bounced off the frontal armor of the German heavy tanks and very often off their thinner side armor. Even the up-gunned M4 Sherman tank armed with a 76mm main gun could not penetrate the front armor of either Tiger

— TIGER —
PLAN OF AMMUNITION STOWAGE

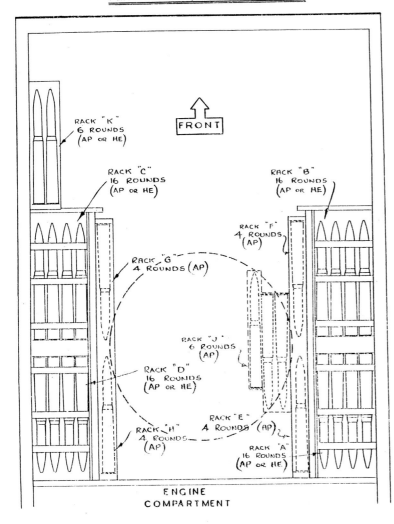

proved later. The Tiger swung back on the narrow road and proceeded about 50 yards (46 meters), then swung his tail to the two tanks. He was then knocked out by an AP through the back plate into the motor. Twenty-four hours later, I had the opportunity to observe the burned Tiger and found the results of the fire.

Several scars were visible on the slope plate (glacis) and around the hull, but the one hit that stood out was a direct hit by an AP to the upper left of the sight opening in the gun shield. The shell had penetrated about five inches straight into the steel and dropped out, doing no damage to the Tiger.

model, except at ranges under 50 yards (46 meters). The ineffectiveness of both the 75mm and 76mm main guns on the M4 Sherman medium tanks is made apparent in the following report in which Sergeant Steward B. Olson describes a battle between several M4 Shermans and a single Tiger B tank:

A Tiger tank coming down from Freialdenhoven to Ederen was spotted by the knocked out, but still manned, mediums (one 75mm and one 76mm). They opened fire at approximately 1000 yards (914 meters), and the Tiger swung to face it. Both tanks got ricochets and direct hits on the Tiger, as

The only American antitank weapon that stood a chance of penetrating the frontal armor on the Tiger B was a modified 90mm antiaircraft gun. The fully tracked M36 Tank Destroyer and the M26 Pershing heavy tank carried these guns. In combat, however, even the 90mm gun proved to be somewhat of a disappointment. Staff Sergeant Harvey W. Anderson, an M4 Sherman medium tank platoon leader, commented on the effectiveness of that gun in a wartime report:

I believe the 90mm gun on the T-26 [M26] is almost comparable to the 88mm on the Mark VI but does not obtain the necessary muzzle velocity to penetrate the Mark V or the VI from the front.

I have actually seen the 90mm armor-piercing cap [APC] bounce off a German VI at about 1400 yards (1,280 meters). In turn, I have seen a

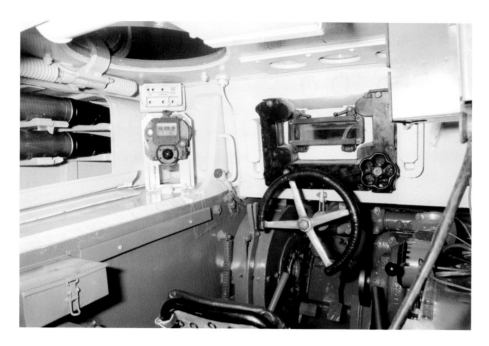

This is a view of the driver's position on the now restored and running Tiger I tank belonging to the Tank Museum. Unlike all the German tanks that came before it, the Tiger I tank had a power-assisted steering wheel that made it very easy to drive the vehicle. To the left of the driver's position was room for six main gun rounds, of which two appear in this picture. *Tank Museum–Bovington*

German Mark VI with an 88mm KO [knock out] an American M4 at 3,300 yards (3,044 meters) with a ricochet hit through the side.

The 90mm M3 shell fired from the M36 tank destroyer and the M26 Pershing heavy tank weighed twenty-four pounds and had more striking energy than the 88mm round fired from the Tiger I or Tiger B tank's main gun.

However, since the quality of the steel used in the round's construction was inferior to what the Germans used, its final performance fell far short of the German main gun AP rounds.

The British army also fielded a large antitank gun that could penetrate the thick armor of Tiger tanks. It was called the 17-pounder (76.2mm) and first entered service in 1942 as a towed antitank gun. A tank-mounted version of the 17-pounder began appearing on American-supplied M4 Sherman medium tanks in British army service just before the Allied invasion of France on June 6, 1944. The British army also mounted the 17-pounder on American-supplied M10 tank destroyers by removing the existing 3-inch main gun that originally came with it.

The British army dubbed the converted Sherman tanks armed with the 17-pounder the "Firefly" and the up-gunned M10 tank destroyers as the "Achilles IIC." The armor-piercing round fired from the 17-pounder could in theory penetrate up to 4.8 inches (120 millimeters) of

On display at a Russian military museum is this thickly armored ISU-152 assault gun-tank destroyer. Intended as a quick fix to counter the Tiger I tank, this turretless vehicle earned the nickname *Zvierboy*— which translates to "Animal Killer"—since its powerful 5.9-inch (152mm) gun made it the only Red Army vehicle that could penetrate the frontal armor on the German heavy tank. *Defense Visual Information System*

steel armor plate at a 30-degree slope at a range of 1,500 yards (1,371 meters). The muzzle velocity of the round was 2,900 feet per second (884.5 meters per second).

SOVIET TIGER KILLERS

At Hitler's insistence, the first production Tiger I tanks were sent into action on the Eastern Front on August 29, 1942. During their first encounter with the Red Army, three of the four Tigers suffered mechanical breakdowns. On September 21, 1942, these same four tanks went into action again, but this time, they were either lost to Soviet antitank guns or became mired in soft ground and were abandoned by their crews. The Germans managed to recover three of the four tanks. The single vehicle not recovered from the battlefield was destroyed in place by its crew to prevent it from falling into Soviet hands.

The Soviets captured their first intact Tiger I on January 16, 1943. After studying their new prize, the Russians realized that much of their inventory of existing tanks and antitank guns was inadequate. To redress this situation, they fielded a variety of turretless self-propelled guns, referred to as "SUs," that carried guns powerful enough to destroy Tiger tanks.

The best-known Red Army SU from World War II, and the most feared by the crews of Tiger tanks, was the SU-152. It was nicknamed "Animal Hunter" or "Conquering Beast" by Soviet soldiers. The vehicle first saw action during the massive tank battle of Kursk in July of

By the summer of 1943, Russian tank designers had identified a need to mount a much larger main gun on their heavy tanks to deal with German Tiger I and Panther tanks. Their answer in early 1944 was to field the roughly 50-ton (45.3-metric ton) IS-2 heavy tank, mounting a 122mm main gun. *Defense Visual Information System*

1943. The 152mm gun mounted on the SU-152 fired a shell that weighed 95 pounds (43 kilograms). The low, 2,000-feet-per-second (610-meters-per-second) muzzle velocity was compensated for by the very high projectile mass. The Soviets fielded 704 of these tank destroyers during World War II.

The U.S. Army's quick fix for dealing with well-armored German tanks like the Tigers and Panther was the fielding of the M36 Tank Destroyer armed with a 90mm main gun in an open-topped turret. The vehicle carried 47 rounds of main gun ammunition that, in theory, could penetrate 6 inches of steel armor at a range of 1,000 yards. *Bob Fleming/ Panzer Prints*

To improve the mobility of its 17-pounder antitank gun, the British army mounted it on a variety of armored full-tracked vehicles, included the M4 Sherman medium tank pictured here. This arrangement made it the most powerful armament installed in the vehicle series during World War II. *Patton Museum*

In late 1943, the Soviet army fielded a heavy tank known as the IS-2 (Iosef Stalin 2), armed with a 122mm main gun. The IS-2 first saw action in February of 1944. It was so effective against German Tiger tanks that Tiger crews sought to engage and destroy IS-2 tanks before engaging any other targets. The Soviets fielded about 3,500 IS-2 tanks during World War II.

TIGER TANK FIREPOWER

Krupp built a 17-foot-long (5.18 meters) version of the 88mm for the Tiger I. Its designation was 8.8cm Kw.K. 36 L/56. Unlike the antiaircraft-gun versions of the 88mm that had percussion-primed ammunition, the Kw.K. 36 employed electric-primed ammunition. (The primer is the component used to ignite the propelling charge of a round.)

The 88mm gun on the Tiger I differed from the antiaircraft versions of the 88mm. Tiger guns were fitted with semi-automatic falling-block vertical breechblocks rather than the horizontal sliding breechblocks of the antiaircraft versions.

The primary tank-killing round fired from the 88mm on the Tiger I tank was designated *Panzergranate 39* (*Pzgr. 39*). Like many World War II German main-gun tank rounds, the 34-pound (15.4kg) *Pzgr. 39* contained a small high-explosive bursting charge with a fuse designed to detonate after the projectile had penetrated the armor of an enemy tank. According to a wartime German army handbook on the Tiger I, the 22.49-pound (10.2-kilogram) *Pzgr. 39* projectile featured a muzzle velocity of 2,657 feet per second (810 meters per second) and could destroy enemy tanks at ranges up to 2,188 yards (2,000 meters).

Another KE tank-killing round fired from the 88mm on the Tiger I tank had the designation *Panzergranate 40* (*Pzgr. 40*). It consisted of a super-hard tungsten sub-caliber core centered within a larger full-bore light-alloy metal body that disintegrated when it struck the target. Because tungsten is harder and denser than steel, it offered a superior level of armor penetration. When fired from the Tiger I tank's 88mm, the *Pzgr. 40* 16-pound (7.3-kilogram) projectile had a muzzle velocity of 3,000 feet per second (915 meters per second). Unlike the *Pzgr. 39*, it did not contain a high-explosive bursting charge.

An Allied intelligence publication dated May 1943 reflects some of the thinking by the British, American, and Red armies regarding German tank-killing ammunition:

The Germans seem to be losing interest in a combination armor-piercing, high-explosive shell, now that substantial thicknesses of armor have to be dealt with. During the past year, they have been improving the anti-armor performance of armor-piercing projectiles: first, by reducing the high

Pz Kpfw 'TIGER I' Ausf. E (mid production)

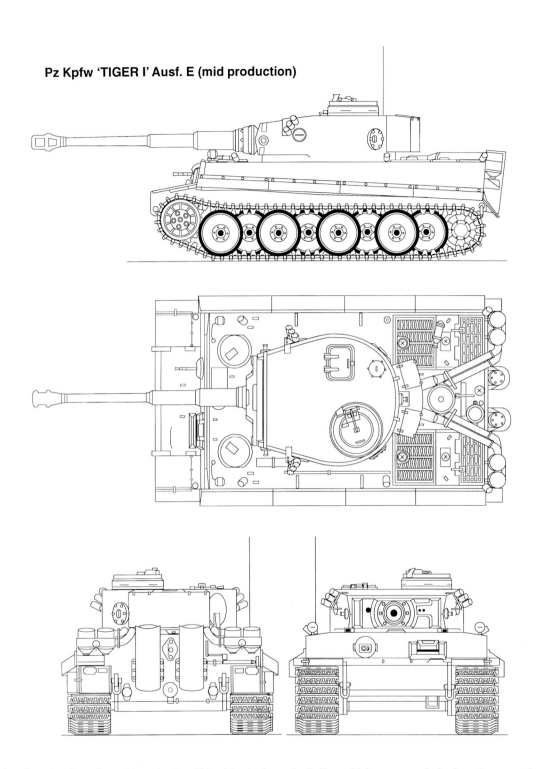

This four-view line drawing of a mid-production Tiger I tank shows both the vehicle commander's drum-type cupola and the loader's hatch on the roof of the vehicle's turret. Visible on the top of the center engine compartment is a large, rectangular door, which allowed access to the engine. Also visible are the heavy-armored grilled plates fitted over the tank's radiators and fan assemblies located on either side of the centrally-mounted engine. *George Bradford*

Pz Kpfw 'TIGER I' Ausf. E (final production)

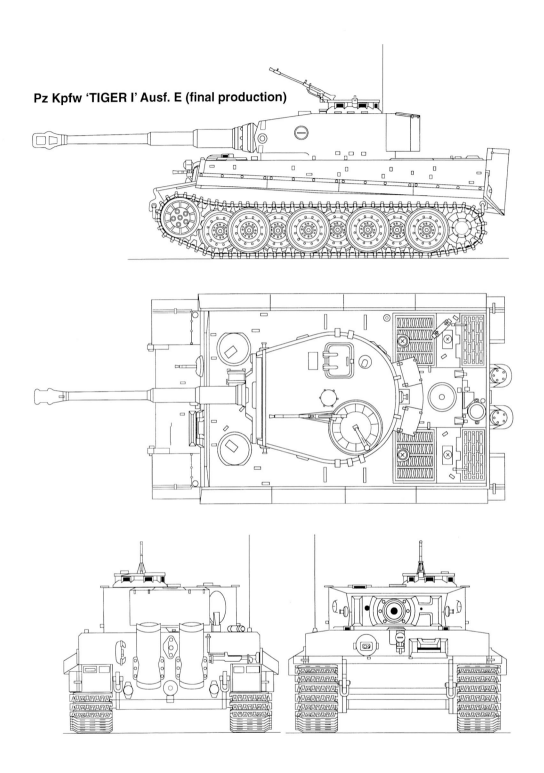

Visible in this four-view line drawing of a late-production Tiger I are the two large external exhaust manifolds on the rear of the tank, a design feature that was carried over from the original prototypes of the vehicle. Production of the Tiger I tank ended in August 1944, by which time 1,350 units of the vehicle had rolled off the assembly line. *George Bradford*

On display at the Tank Museum in Bovington is this Tiger B with one of the original 50 Porsche-designed turrets. Notice the curved front and side plates of the vehicle's turret not seen on the Henschel-designed turret, which had a near-vertical front turret armor plate through which the main gun protruded. Also noticeable in this picture is another characteristic of the Porsche turret—the protrusion in the side wall to accommodate the vehicle commander's position. *Tank Museum–Bovington*

explosive capacity of the heavier armor-piercing shells and, second, by continuing to develop high-velocity, armor-piercing shot with a tungsten carbide core. What this amounts to is that the Germans are employing shot for attack against thick armor, while retaining, for every weapon, high-explosive shells to be used in attacks against 'thin-skinned' targets.

The Germans also fired a shaped-charge high-explosive antitank (HEAT) round weighing 29 pounds (13.17 kilograms) known as the *Granate 39 HL* (or *HL. GR. Patr.*) from the 88mm on the Tiger I.

The official storage arrangement on the Tiger I provided space for 92 maingun rounds within the vehicle's hull. A captured German non-commissioned officer who served on Tiger I tanks divulged the following information concerning the vehicle's ammunition storage arrangement:

A prisoner stated that his Pz.Kw. VI carried over 100 shells for the gun, "stowed everywhere,"

This is a side view of a captured German army Tiger B tank fitted with one of the original 50 Porsche-designed turrets. This picture clearly shows the curved lower front portion of the turret and the vehicle commander's position that protrudes outward from the side of the turret wall. The Tiger B was almost 33 feet (10.06 meters) long with the main gun pointed forward and about 24 feet (7.31 meters) long excluding the main gun. *Tank Museum–Bovington*

American soldiers are taking a captured Tiger B out for a test drive. The various white stars attached to the turret and front superstructure/hull plate are to let everybody in the area know not to open fire upon the vehicle. The Tiger B had a width of almost 12 feet (3.66 meters) and was just a bit over 10 feet (3.05 meters) high. *Patton Museum*

however, the standard ammunition load is 92 shells. According to him, although the 88mm gun in the Pz.Kw. VI can fire up to 10,000 to 12,000 yards (9,140 to 10,968 meters) indirect, this type of firing is very difficult and is seldom undertaken. He declared that the best range is 1,000 to 2,000 yards (914 to 1,828 meters), "the nearer the better."

For dealing with enemy infantry and non-armored vehicles, the 88mm on the Tiger I tank was provided with a 31.7-pound (14.4-kilogram) HE round referred to in the German language as *Sprenggranate*. In text, it was normally shortened to just *Sprgr.* The projectile portion of the *Sprgr.* weighed 19.8 pounds (9 kilograms).

TIGER B MAIN-GUN ROUNDS

Like the Tiger I, the Tiger B featured an 88mm as its main gun. However, the gun tube on the Tiger B was 3 feet 7 inches (109.2 centimeters) longer than the gun tube on the Tiger I and boasted a dramatic increase in performance compared to its shorter counterpart. Designated the 8.8cm Kw.K. 43 L/71, it came with a large, double-baffle muzzle brake similar to that on the Tiger I. The ammunition for this new version of the 88mm was longer, heavier, and more powerful than that fired from the 88mm on the Tiger I tank.

An article from a January 1945 issue of the *Intelligence Bulletin* describes just how impressive the performance was of the new 88mm on the Tiger B:

> *German experiences with Soviet heavy tanks have resulted in the production of some very powerful guns. Among these is the Model 1943 88mm gun. This improved 88mm has a very high muzzle velocity, which enables gunners to lay [aim] on and hit even distant moving targets with considerable ease. In fact, the trajectory followed by the projectile is so flat that, with certain sights, the gunner can make his own elevation calculations up to a range of 3,700 yards (3,482 meters) for high explosive projectiles and 4,400 yards (4,058 meters) for armor-piercing projectiles. A trajectory as flat as this naturally means that gunners can open fire on tanks and other armored vehicles without preliminary registration. The rise of the shell in its flight seldom will be greater than the height of a tank.*

The primary antitank round for the 88mm on the Tiger B was the 34.35-pound (15.6-kilogram) *Pzgr. 39/43*. In flight, the 22.44-pound (10.2-kilogram) projectile, which contained a small high-explosive charge, featured a muzzle velocity of 3,280 feet per second (1,000 meters per second) and, in theory, could penetrate steel armor 5.69 inches (132 millimeters) thick sloped at 30 degrees at a range of 2,188 yards (2,000 meters).

Like the 88mm on the Tiger I tank, the 88mm on the Tiger B went into combat with two other armor-penetrating rounds. They included the 27.91-pound (12.7-kilogram) *Pzgr. 40/43* with the sub-caliber tungsten core and the 28.74-pound (13-kilogram) *Gr. 39/43 HL* (*hohlgranate*, or hollow charge in English) with a shaped-charged warhead.

The 16-pound (7.2-kilogram) projectile of the *Pzgr. 40/43* had a muzzle velocity of 3,775 feet per second (1,151 meters per second) and, in theory, could penetrate 6.12 inches (153 millimeters) of steel armor sloped at 30 degrees at a range of 2,188 yards (2,000 meters). The 16.83-pound (7.6-kilogram) projectile of the *Gr. 39/43*

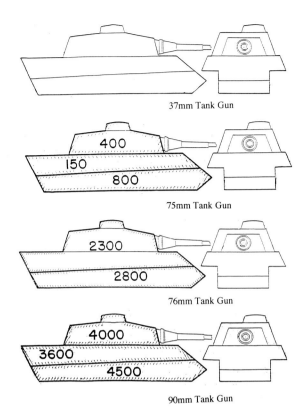

37mm Tank Gun

75mm Tank Gun

76mm Tank Gun

90mm Tank Gun

Prepared by the Technical Section of the U.S. Army's Ordnance Branch in January 1945, these line drawings of the Tiger B show its vulnerability, or lack thereof, to a number of American tank main guns at their maximum range, in yards, at which penetration of different plates is likely to occur. The ranges shown were computed based on a zero angle of attack. *National Archives*

HL had a muzzle velocity of only 1,980 feet per second (604 meters per second) and could theoretically penetrate steel armor 3.6 inches (90 millimeters) thick sloped at 30 degrees when fired at a target 2,188 yards (2,000 meters). It contained no HE element. Besides the various tank-killing main gun rounds, the 88mm on the Tiger could fire a standard *Sprgr.* HE round for use against infantry and non-armored vehicles.

A U.S. Army report dated September 13, 1944, described details of the 88mm on the Tiger B:

> *An official German document states that the gun has an elevation of 15 degrees and a depression of eight degrees. . . . The length of the ordnance*

from rear of the breech ring to end of barrel is 20 feet 8 inches (6.3 meters . . . . And, air blast (i.e., bore evacuator) is fitted, consisting of nozzles arranged each side of the breech ring to direct jets of air into the chamber and prevent flame or gases passing back into the turret while the breech is open.

GUN OPTICS

One of the major contributing factors leading to the success of the 88mm as an antitank weapon in World War II was the weapon's outstanding optics (sights). The

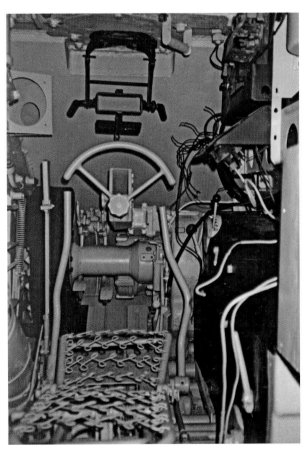

This picture shows the driver's position of the Tiger B now on display at the Patton Museum of Armor and Cavalry. Notice the bracket for holding the driver's 360-degree rotating periscope and the handles used for turning it. The driver's seat on the Tiger B adjusted so that he could drive "closed-down" (lower position) or "opened up" with his head and shoulders outside the hatch (upper position). *Patton Museum*

While both the Tiger I and Tiger B tanks featured the 88mm gun as their main armament, they featured different versions of the weapon. Nothing better illustrates the increased power and penetrative ability of the 88mm projectile fired from the Kw.K. 43 mounted on the Tiger B than a comparison of the size of their main armor-piercing (AP) rounds. The round fired from the Tiger I tank's main gun is on the right and that of the Tiger B on the left. *Michael Green*

In Roberts Ick's book *Famous Tank Battles,* there is a description of Tiger I tank tactics in Russia in which they used their long-range firepower advantage to slow down advancing Soviet armored forces:

> *Most of the Russian tank losses occurred as a result of following too closely the elements of the German rearguards. Often these rearguard units consisted only of a few infantry or combat engineers riding on a Tiger tank. Defilade positions or locations just inside an orchard or woods would be prepared, and when Russian tanks exposed themselves, the Tigers, with their longer-range 88mm guns, would pick them off, usually concentrating on tanks behind the leading Russian tanks, throwing the leading tanks into confusion and quick retirement. The Tigers then would move off to the west a few miles to repeat the action.*

TIGER FIRE-CONTROL SYSTEMS

Early tank designs had been fitted with straight-through telescopic sights attached directly to a tank's main gun. While simple in design, this type of arrangement was very awkward for tank gunners. Whenever the main gun barrel moved in elevation, the gunner had to manually follow the barrel with the sight.

The gunner on most Tiger I tanks had an articulated binocular (two-lens) telescopic sight known as the TZF 9b, with the gunner's eyepiece remaining in a fixed position despite movement of the tank's main gun. The TZF 9b sight had a magnification of 2.5-power. Beginning in April 1944, the Tiger I Ausf. E got a monocular (single-lens) TZF 9c sight that had two magnifications, including 2.5-power and 5-power.

All Tiger B tanks with the standard-production Henschel turret were fitted with a monocular (single-lens) telescopic sight known as the TZF 9d. This sighting system gave the Tiger B gunner a choice between 3-power or 6-power optics. The 6-power magnification was employed for acquiring longer-range targets, while the 3-power magnification was for closer-range targets. The first 50 Tiger B tanks built with the Porsche turret were fitted with the binocular TZF 9b sight. Some were later rebuilt with the monocular TZF 9d telescopic sight.

All versions of the TZF 9 sights fitted on the Tiger I and Tiger B were limited to a field of view of roughly 23 degrees. This somewhat limited field of view was

battlefield effectiveness of any gun in direct-fire mode depends on the crew's ability to spot a target, engage it, and then destroy it in the shortest amount of time possible. Because the German optics industry was the best in the world prior to World War II, German antitank guns had the ability to see and engage opponents at ranges far greater than their Allied counterparts.

Normally outnumbered, German Tiger tank crews used their long-range firepower advantage to reduce the number of attacking enemy tanks before they could get within the effective engagement range of their own weapons.

common for tanks of the World War II era. Because of the better overall view from the top of a tank, target acquisition and initial range-determination is normally the responsibility of the tank commander, although he is frequently assisted by other crew members.

The tank commander is usually the first crewman to see a target. Upon spotting a target, a typical Tiger commander would give directions to his gunner over the intercom regarding the location and approximate range of the target. The gunner would then turn the turret and gun to the general direction of the target. Once the target appeared in the gunner's sight, he would announce it to the tank commander over the intercom.

The gunner's sight contained two illuminated transparent discs (a feature also found on the Pz.Kfpw. IV and Panther), with the first having a range scale inscribed around its circumference. The gunner turned this disc until the appropriate range to a target was set against a small pointer. This action would simultaneously raise the other transparent disc, which incorporated the gunner's graticules (aiming grids in any type of sighting device). The gunner would then overlay the aiming marks on the target using his hand-operated elevation and traverse controls. If the gunner knew the width of the target, he could make a fairly accurate range determination. This range estimate is known as a stadiametric range determining system. Most World War II tank commanders' binoculars featured a stadiametric range scale.

OPTICAL RANGEFINDERS

Tiger tank crews often carried in their vehicles a small, hand-held coincidence rangefinder, designated the TZR l, to assist in the observation and ranging of targets. It had an overall length of 55 inches (140 centimeters) and a field of view of six degrees. Tiger tank commanders used it to see over the flash or muzzle obscuration (dust) generated by the firing of the main gun.

Early-production Tiger I tanks with the drum-pattern cupola did not have the bracket for mounting the TZR l. Instead, the crew used a hand-held optical rangefinder similar to those used by the crews of German antiaircraft guns.

In a coincidence rangefinder, the distance to the target is measured by sighting on the target and bringing the erect image into coincidence with the inverted image in

On display at the German Tank Museum are two main gun rounds fired from the 88mm gun mounted in the Tiger B. The Germans color-coded their rounds to make it easier for the crews to identify the correct one in the heat of battle. The standard armor-piercing round on the Tiger B was designated *Panzergrante 39/42* and featured a black nose with a white tip. Those with yellow noses signified they were high-explosive (HE) rounds.
Frank Schulz

the field of view. The range is then read on a range scale. Coincidence rangefinders work very well under conditions of clear visibility and especially well for sharply defined objects. They are ineffective at longer ranges and for targets having indistinct outlines. They are also easy to use, requiring only a couple of hours of instruction to achieve competency.

U.S. Army Lieutenant Colonel Wilson M. Hawkins, commanding the 3rd Battalion, 67th Armored Regiment, wrote in a wartime report about his opinion of German tank sights, "The matter of tank gun sights has caused us much concern. I have looked through and worked with sights in German Mark V (Panther) and Mark VI (Tiger)

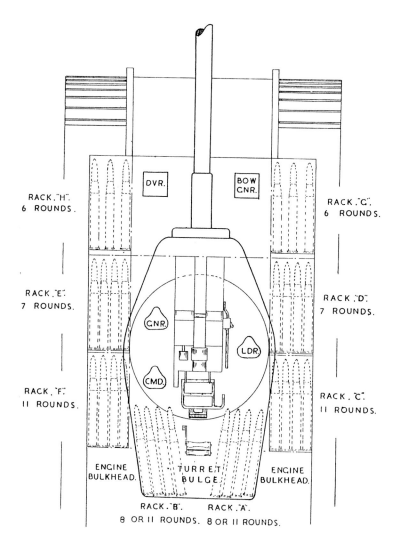

ROYAL TIGER.
PLAN OF AMMUNITION STOWAGE.

RACK "H".
6 ROUNDS.

RACK "E".
7 ROUNDS.

RACK "F".
II ROUNDS.

DVR.

BOW
CNR.

CNR.

LDR.

CMD.

ENGINE
BULKHEAD.

TURRET
BULGE.

ENGINE
BULKHEAD.

RACK "G".
6 ROUNDS.

RACK "D".
7 ROUNDS.

RACK "C".
II ROUNDS.

RACK "B".   RACK "A".
8 OR II ROUNDS. 8 OR II ROUNDS.

From a 1947 British Army report comes this overhead line drawing showing the placement of main gun rounds in the superstructure/ hull and turret of the Tiger B. Some Tiger B crews decided to store all their main gun rounds within the lower superstructure/ hull and not to store any rounds in the rear turret bustle racks, since they were more vulnerable there. *Tank Museum–Bovington*

tanks as well as our own. I find that the German sight has more magnifying power and clearness than our own, which is a big advantage to a gunner."

BACKUP FIRE CONTROL SYSTEMS

The Tiger gunner's firing accuracy was improved by an illuminated inclinometer on his right side. This device is used to measure angles from horizontal. In artillery pieces and tank guns, the inclinometer is used to correct barrel elevation if the gun carriage is not exactly level. In American military terms, the device is known as a quadrant.

A traverse (turret position) indicator driven by a pinion from the turret was mounted to the left of the Tiger I gunner. It was marked with a counter-rotating clock-like device graded from 1 o'clock to 12 o'clock. The arm for the 12 o'clock position was fixed in place to indicate the forward direction of the vehicle's hull. When the gunner moved the vehicle's turret (when tracking a moving target for example), the second hand of the position indicator measured the azimuth position of the main gun. The tank commander had a matching counter-rotating azimuth indicator (fitted around the interior of his cupola on a toothed annular ring) to follow the gunner's actions.

A simple blade foresight mounted in front of the Tiger I tank commander's station gave the commander a very basic and crude aiming device. The Tiger B commander had an improved, but still crude, aiming device. By dropping or raising his head within the confines of his cupola, he could look out through a blade sight attached to the forward cupola periscope and quickly determine what his gunner was looking at (or should be looking at). Because the Tiger B tank commander could easily observe his gunner's traverse indicator device from his position, the matching counter-rotating azimuth indicator seen on the Tiger I tank does not appear on the Tiger B tank.

A destroyed Tiger B sits in a German street with an American soldier climbing out of the tank, no doubt looking for souvenirs. The penetration hole on the side of the turret that knocked out this tank is clearly visible. British army tests on the Tiger B showed that the tank's design offered a very reasonable amount of comfort to all the crew members except for the gunner. *Tank Museum–Bovington*

According to gunnery test results conducted by the British on captured Tiger I tanks and later supplied to the U.S. Army, the sighting systems resulted in excellent firing accuracy for the 88mm gun on the Tiger I. The results state, "A five-round grouping of 16 inches by 18 inches (40.6 by 45.7 centimeters) was obtained at a range of 1,200 yards (1,097 meters). Five rounds were fired at targets moving at 15 miles per hour (24 kilometers per hour) and, although smoke obscured observation by the gunner, three hits were scored after directions were given by the commander. Normal rate of fire was estimated to be from five to eight rounds per minute.

SECONDARY ARMAMENT

In addition to their 88mm main guns, the Tiger I and Tiger B were fitted with up to three 7.92mm machine guns. Both models of the Tiger had a machine gun fixed to fire alongside the tank's main gun. In military terms, this is known as a coaxial machine gun (or coax). The gunner on the Tiger tank controlled both the aiming and firing of the tank's coax. The gunner actually fired the gun mechanically with a foot pedal. It was up to the tank's loader to keep the weapon loaded and operational.

Both the Tiger I and Tiger B also featured a front-hull-mounted 7.92mm machine gun operated by the radioman, aimed with the aid of a small optical sight and fired by a hand trigger. Because the front-hull machine gun itself was breech-heavy, it was balanced by an equilibrator spring. In its ball mounting, this weapon could be elevated to 20 degrees, depressed to 10 degrees, and had a traverse of 15 degrees both left and right. The *Tiger Primer* describes which targets this gun was most effective against: "Hull machine gun up to 200 meters (219 yards) against men, horses, and vehicles. Turret machine gun up to 400 meters (438 yards) against men, horses, and vehicles. If there's a lot of them, then at greater ranges. Also for occupied houses and for enemy soldiers lying prone on the ground."

Both the Tiger I with the late-model cupola and the Tiger B had an attachment rail on the tank commander's cupola for the mounting of an additional 7.92mm machine gun. Because this weapon could be used independently of the Tiger's main gun and coax, the vehicle commander could engage a second target while his gunner was firing at the first. Like the coax gun, it was also useful for firing at infantry or unarmored vehicles. However, it was almost useless against armored Allied ground-attack aircraft.

The 7.92mm machine guns mounted on the Tiger tanks and all other German medium tanks was the *Maschinengewehr* 34 (MG34). First accepted for German

On display at the German Tank Museum is this Tiger B with a late-war camouflage paint scheme. The glacis plate on the tank was 5.9 inches (150 millimeters) thick and sloped at 50 degrees, while the rounded mantlet on the front of the turret ranged in thickness from 2 inches to 3.2 inches (50 to 80 millimeters). *Frank Schulz*

army service in 1934, it did not reach production until 1936. A first-class weapon, the MG34 had a very high rate of fire of 750 rounds per minute. Both the coaxial and hull-mounted MG34 machine guns on the Tiger came with a spare-parts box that contained two spare barrels, a bipod, and a stock for dismounted use. The tank commander's machine gun on Tigers could also be an improved wartime model known as the MG42.

In addition to the crew's individual pistols, there was normally a single MP38 or MP40 model submachine gun, incorrectly known to most Allied soldiers as the "Schmeisser," in both the Tiger I and Tiger B turrets. It was also nicknamed the "Burp gun" by many Allied soldiers. It saw use for guard duty by the crew if there was no infantry support, or as a close-in defense weapon of last resort. In the last year of the war in Europe, Tiger tanks had their MP38/40 submachine guns replaced by the far superior StG44 assault rifle.

Tiger I Primer stated, regarding the crew's hand-held weapons, "Use pistols from the pistol port against guests

on the hull. Submachine guns can also be used out of the pistol port against emplacements and machine gun nests in the dead zone. Eggs (grenades) out of the pistol port against foxholes and concealed targets."

There were two small pistol ports in early versions of the Tiger I turret, reduced to one in later models. Porsche-designed Tiger B turrets were fitted with a single small gun port on the left side, later welded over. The standard-production turret for the Tiger B had no provisions for the firing of small arms from within the vehicle. Instead, a small armored hatch on top of the turret was designed to mount the same multi-purpose 360-degree rotating grenade launcher that appeared on some Tiger I tanks. This device did not appear on all Tiger B tanks due to shortages of the device.

TIGER TANK MOBILITY

Mobility is almost as important as firepower and armor protection to a tank's success on the battlefield. Mobility includes strategic mobility (the ability to move rapidly into a zone of operation), operational mobility (the ability to move rapidly around a zone of operation once the tank has gotten there), and tactical or battlefield mobility (the ability to move quickly to firing positions and evade enemy fire).

A crucial factor in battlefield mobility is a tank's endurance. This includes both operating range (a factor of fuel capacity and consumption) and operating distance between breakdowns (expressed in statistical terms as mean miles between failure). Endurance is based largely on the moving parts in the propulsion system and running gear. These components naturally include the engine, transmission, tracks, track drives/supports, and wheels.

Maybach aircraft engines specially modified for tank usage propelled all World War II German medium and heavy tanks. These water-cooled gasoline-powered V-12 engines came in several power ratings. Early-model Tiger I tanks had a Maybach HL 210 21-liter engine rated at 650 horsepower. This engine was soon upgraded in production to the HL 230 23-liter engine rated at 700 horsepower. The HL 230 later appeared in both the Panther tank and the Tiger B tank.

TIGER COMBAT MOBILITY

Many people perceive the Tiger I and Tiger B as being slow and unwieldy because of their size and weight. This was not completely true. For their day and the roles they were designed to fill, the Tiger tanks did fairly well in some circumstances, when compared to many Allied tanks. U.S. Army Captain Henry W. Johnson, of the 2nd Armored Division, recounted in a report:

> The wider tracks of the Mark V and the Mark VI enable it to move much better cross-country and in muddy or snow-covered terrain than the narrow tracks of the Sherman tank. The field expedient of duck bills added to widen the Sherman tread aids [mobility], but does not effect [sic] the advantage the German Mark V and Mark VI tanks have. It is my opinion that the Mark V and Mark VI enemy tanks are far superior in maneuverability to our Sherman tanks.
>
> The slow cruising speed of the German tanks enables them to move into position and to slip up on our tanks much easier than the loud noise of our own motors will enable us to move.

Staff Sergeant Alvin G. Olson, a tank platoon leader in the 2nd Armored Division, stated in a wartime report, "At Freialdenhoven, Germany, I saw a Mark V and Mark VI tank scarcely dig into the plowed field while the tracks of our M4 tanks were often deep enough in the same field to show the marks of the tank's belly dragging."

The capability of a tank to traverse soft soils without sinking depends on a number of interrelated factors. Tank engineers design for the lowest ground pressure. The heavier a tank becomes, the wider and longer its tracks need to be. The objective is to distribute the weight over a large enough area to allow the vehicle to "float" on soft terrains. Tiger tracks were wide, and the vehicle was long, so it had relatively low ground pressure.

Another factor that contributes to soft-soil mobility (part of what is now called trafficability) is the weight distribution. Excess weight in the front, back, or either side of the vehicle raises the ground pressure at those locations and can cause a corner of the vehicle to sink in mud or other soft terrains. The vehicle can be immobilized if this happens. The Tigers were fairly well balanced.

A third factor is traction. Tank tracks are designed to aggressively clutch the ground so that they do not slip.

Finally, a lot of power is required to displace mud and soft sand at high speeds. The power-to-weight ratio and design details of the Tiger suspensions allowed them to traverse muddy European fields at much higher speeds

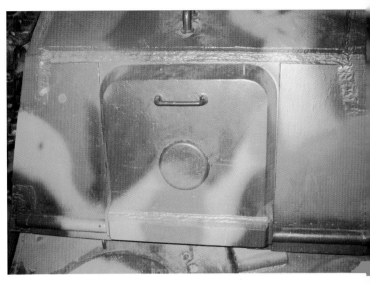

At the rear of the Tiger B turret is a large, rectangular hatch, pictured here, that has a small pistol port in the middle. The British army referred to it as a rear escape hatch. However, they discovered that when the racks in the rear turret bustle were fully stored with main gun rounds, leaving the vehicle's turret by that route was almost impossible for even the thinnest crew member. *Frank Schulz*

than the lighter-weight Allied tanks. The Tigers consistently surprised American tankers who were unable to cross the same muddy European fields that the Tigers glided over with ease. The Tigers' advanced (for their day) torsion bar suspension provided high road-wheel travel capable of absorbing large terrain features at high speeds. Cross-country speed capability was also enhanced by the vehicle's long hull, which minimized pitching motion.

MOBILITY PROBLEMS

The Tiger I and Tiger B had their automotive weaknesses. These were more pronounced in the Tiger B because of its greater weight. The Germans were always less concerned with mechanical reliability than the U.S. Army, and, as a result, were always in desperate need of replacement tanks. They tended to rush their tanks almost straight from the drawing board to the battlefield. Hitler's personal interest in the Tiger tanks and his demands that they be fielded quickly also caused problems. This policy resulted in numerous automotive teething problems in the field, which, in turn, required an almost continuous series of minor modifications to keep the vehicles running properly.

U.S. Army Colonel William A. Hamberg (retired), who commanded a tank battalion from the famous 5th Armored Division during World War II, remembers, "Almost half the Tiger tanks we ran into during our drive across Europe were abandoned either due to mechanical problems or lack of fuel."

The weight, power, and fuel storage capacity of German tanks limited the operating range to about 85 miles. When traveling cross-country, the range of the Tigers could drop to forty miles or less. Franz Kutz, who fought on the Russian front as a German infantryman and is familiar with the Tiger's range problem, recalls, "I was always very happy to see our tanks, especially Tigers. The only problem was their very short range, which meant they would always leave us when we needed them the most. When in battle with Russian tanks, I always preferred the support of our *Sturmgeschutz* (full-tracked assault guns often used as tank destroyers) who almost always stayed with us."

The following comments on the Tiger tanks' range problems are contained in an article by U.S. Lieutenant Colonel Albin F. Irzyk (U.S. Army) in the January 1946 issue of the *Military Review*:

It might astonish some to know that [German] prisoners of war claimed that some of their large tanks had a running time of a mere two and a half hours on a full vehicular load of gasoline. Thus, the tanks did not have the endurance nor the cruising ranges of our tanks (M4 Sherman medium tanks). Therefore, in many instances they had to be transported by rail virtually to the front lines, unloaded, and put into the battle. How far could we have gone with our tanks if we had had to follow a procedure like that?

The short operational range of the German tanks was common with many Allied tanks of World War II. Volume under armor is very limited in a tank, and fuel takes up a lot of room that would be better utilized for such things as ammunition. Large onboard fuel stores are also dangerous if the armor of a tank is pierced. Thus, it is critical that large amounts of fuel be available near the front lines to support the tanks. This was a problem for the Germans; their logistical support units were under continuous air attack for much of the later part of World War II. Without an uninterrupted fuel supply, the best tank in the world becomes nothing more than an expensive bunker. Tanks have a short life span. Owing to their heavy armor and the necessity to use small, lightweight engines, suspension components, and running gear to conserve space for potent weapons and onboard ammunition, the automotive components and running gear are always under high stress. Even in peacetime, it is not unusual for a tank to require a major overhaul after less than six thousand miles of use.

The German army was well aware of the limitations of their Tiger tanks. Special instructions were issued to upper-level German officers to remind them that the Tiger tank could turn the tide of battle in their favor as

The only U.S. Army tank in World War II that stood a chance of defeating German tanks like the Tiger I and the Panther from the front was the 46-ton (41.7-metric ton) M26 Pershing heavy tank armed with a powerful 90mm main gun. Sadly, it appeared in service only during the last few months of the war in Europe.
Patton Museum

A Tiger B on display at the U.S. Army Ordnance Museum in the early 1960s. During the Vietnam War, the U.S. Army needed the building where the museum's collection of historical vehicles was housed and forced the bulk of the collection outside, where it has been subjected to the ravages of the weather for many decades. Fortunately, this Tiger B was transferred to the Patton Museum, were it now resides on display indoors. *Ordnance Museum*

long as they used them sparingly. For example, forced marches were forbidden, since they placed undue strain on the engine, transmission, and suspension systems. Tiger tank tracks, which were made of cast manganese (as were all German tank tracks before and during World War II), had a life span of less than 500 miles (804.5 kilometers) when subjected to hard use. When Tigers were forced to move from one battlefield position to another, the instructions suggested that they travel individually. Traveling alone, a tank can be driven at steady speeds with minimal use of the clutch and brakes, thereby saving wear and tear on critical components.

Because of their size and weight, the route of Tiger tanks had to be planned very carefully. Terrain features, bridges, manmade structures, and, of course, minefields all had to be taken into account. A number of postwar memoirs by German officers mention the necessity of changing their battle plans to accommodate the tactical and terrain limitations of the Tiger tanks.

Dr. Wolfgang Sterner, who commanded a variety of German medium tanks in World War II, discussed his opinion of the Tiger tanks, which he first saw in the summer of 1943, saying, "They were certainly impressive tanks. The Tiger was a tremendous fighting machine. On the other hand, it was a slow tank. We saw them creeping along. Other disadvantages [include their being] too heavy for bridges. For myself, I would not have volunteered for a Tiger, because for me, in combat, speed was one of the most important things in those days. Hitting power and speed meant for me much more than thick armor."

Charles Lemons, the curator of the Patton Museum of Cavalry and Armor, sums up his impression of the Tiger B on display at his museum:

In general, this was one dangerous vehicle. For its size and weight, it was much more maneuverable than most Allied tanks, and was capable of handling any vehicle sent against it. Mechanically, it had some major problems, which could have been solved had time been available. The final drives on each side were its 'Achilles heel,' and many of [the Tigers] had to be abandoned because of it.

Its other problems would include things that you normally wouldn't think of or directly connected to the vehicle. Support, in the form of transport and recovery, was really lacking. The only vehicle capable of recovering a Tiger was another Tiger. It had problems in rail transportation, and many small bridges could not handle the weight. This severely restricted where the vehicle could go. On the road, it was slower than the mediums, but not that much slower. It was because the vehicle required special considerations when crossing bridges that columns were slowed by it. Fuel consumption was excessive with the Tiger, and the vehicle was underpowered for its weight. Fire control and sighting was superior to [those of] the Allies, and if infrared sighting had been introduced, it would have made the vehicle even more dangerous on the defensive.

INDEX

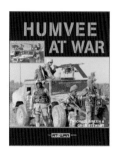
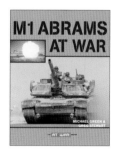
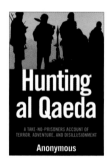
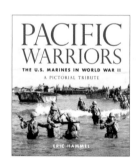